Getting Started with Grails

Written by:
Jason Rudolph

C4Media, Publisher of InfoQ.com.

This book is part of the InfoQ Enterprise Software Development series of books.

For information or ordering of this or other InfoQ books, please contact books@c4media.com.

Managing Editor: Floyd Marinescu
Cover art: Gene Steffanson
Composition: Laura Brown

Library of Congress Cataloguing-in-Publication Data:

ISBN: 978-1-4303-0782-2

Printed in the United States of America

Acknowledgements

I would like to thank Graeme Rocher (Grails project lead and author of *The Definitive Guide to Grails*) for reviewing this book and for enlightening me to the inner workings of Grails along the way. Your detailed review provided invaluable technical insight and excellent recommendations for incorporating "Groovier" solutions into the examples.

I would also like to thank Venkat Subramaniam (co-author of *Practices of an Agile Developer*) for reviewing this book with a keen emphasis on the learning experience and how to best introduce Grails to the reader. In addition to that contribution, your insightful foreword welcomes developers to a framework that will surely foster agility and its many benefits.

I'd like to thank Steve Rollins for diligently pouring through this book to uncover any lingering issues, even though it meant a few weeks of being a nerd outside of normal working hours. Your tireless attention to detail is clearly reflected in the final product.

I would also like to thank Jared Richardson (co-author of *Ship it! A Practical Guide to Successful Software Projects*) not only for reviewing this book, but for motivating me to write it in the first place. Your encouragement throughout the process and your valuable perspective on the end result are greatly appreciated.

I would like to thank Floyd Marinescu (co-founder of InfoQ.com and author of *EJB Design Patterns*) and the entire team at InfoQ for publishing this book and for your enthusiastic support throughout the effort.

Most importantly, I'd like to thank my unflinchingly patient and encouraging wife Michelle for supporting me throughout this effort. It was only by your willingness to do far more than your fair share (of just about everything) that I was able to have time for this project. And as if it wasn't enough just to provide the support to make this book possible, your creativity, sense of style, and editorial input contributed to make this book better than it would have been on its own.

Contents

Foreword

Those of us keen on developing software applications will find that Agile Development greatly improves our chances of success. But, what's agility? At its core, it starts with developing a relatively small feature and quickly getting feedback from our customers. They tell us if we're on the right track, help us develop what's relevant to them, and together we make sure we're constructing an application that will add value to their business. Why should we be agile? As an industry, we've spent far too long watching other development methodologies fail to deliver systems that truly satisfy the customer's needs. To ultimately deliver what our customers want, we need to take smaller and quicker steps, and touch base with our customers frequently to deliver useful features that they can exercise and critique.

Two key things influence our ability to be agile.

First, it's the attitude of everyone involved. The attitude of each person on a team, and the team as a whole, has a significant impact on all aspects of a project. Attitude determines how willing we are to closely cooperate with other developers and with customers, to seek their feedback, and to use that feedback to improve our work.

Second, it's the languages, frameworks, and tools we use to get our work done. Our chosen technologies must enable us to quickly create useful code and to afford quick change in response to customer feedback.

Some languages and frameworks require developers to go though a remarkable amount of effort before they can produce useful executable code. You may have to muddle though XML configuration files, implement an exhaustive set of interfaces, and perform certain operations repeatedly at different layers of your application. In this environment, it often requires an inordinate amount of effort before you can see the working results of any changes. Once you finally create working code, the mere thought of introducing change may put you off from ever even soliciting feedback. A subconscious resistance to change soon ensues, and pleasing the customer suddenly takes a back seat to avoiding change.

Fortunately, we've seen some languages and frameworks emerge in recent years that support a more agile development approach. They allow you to create working, demonstrable code in minutes, not days or weeks, and still ensure the quality of that code. And when you get that valuable feedback from your customers, these languages and frameworks tend to facilitate change, not obstruct it.

How exactly does that work? First, these frameworks follow the DRY (Don't Repeat Yourself) principle. Because each aspect of your application exists in a single location, you don't have to modify multiple layers of code to effect a change. Instead, you make your change in one place and, for the most part, you're done. Second, they follow a convention-over-configuration strategy, so you don't have to spend time explaining the obvious; instead, you get straight to writing useful, productive code. Third, they're lightweight; you can change a particular piece of code and see the results of that change reflected immediately, without explicit recompilation or slow and burdensome redeployments.

That sounds intriguing, but, you may ask, "Where does that leave all the investments we've made in other languages and frameworks, like Java, Hibernate, Spring, etc.?" That's where Grails comes in. Because Grails makes use of the Groovy language (which runs on the JVM), it allows you to integrate with as much Java code as you like, so you can still leverage your current investments. As you explore Grails, you will find that it makes use of good, practical principles – it exercises convention-over-configuration, honors the DRY principle, and is overall lightweight – making it a sound agile framework. But don't take my word for it. Follow along with the examples that Jason has created for you, code along as you read, and see for yourself how Grails contributes to your agility. Then, find a partner, pick an area of your application, and give it a try!

Venkat Subramaniam
November 2006

Speak properly, and in as few words as you can, but always plainly;
for the end of speech is not ostentation, but to be understood.
  - William Penn

Example is not the main thing in influencing others. It is the only
thing.
  - Albert Schweitzer

1

Introduction

Grails is an open-source web application framework that's all about getting things done.

A university professor once assured me – actually he tried his darndest to ingrain it in all his students – that the best software engineers are out of the office and on the golf course by 10 a.m. Why? Because they're focused, efficient, and productive developers. Surely the proposition of calling it a day before the coffee is cold seems unlikely, but wouldn't it be nice to have a typical day's worth of work done before your second cup?

Ruby on Rails pioneered the innovative coupling of a powerful programming language and an opinionated framework that favors sensible defaults over complex configuration. Developers praise the revolutionary Rails framework (and rightfully so) for its revival of productivity, but many organizations aren't yet ready to stray from the safety of Java. So if we can achieve similar productivity and (*shhhh!*) fun with a more Java-centric solution, what's not to like? Grails makes that idea a reality. And the more conservative businesses should find additional comfort knowing that Grails applications play nicely with their existing Java code, because Grails applications are written in Groovy – a dynamically-typed scripting language that stands to soon become a Java standard.[1]

Grails embraces convention over configuration, a technique that facilitates both focus and productivity. Convention dictates where each component belongs in an application, how it's named, and how it interacts with other components. In short, developers know exactly where to place a given component and what it should be called, and new team members will know just where to find that component, all by convention.

Groovy provides a highly-expressive and fully object-oriented language for building Grails applications. Groovy allows the developer to convey ideas concisely and naturally, in a manner that's easy to read and understand. And, Java developers will appreciate its familiar syntax and its seamless Java integration, knowing that they can invoke any Java class from within Groovy, and vice versa.

At its foundation, Grails is supported by proven technologies. Hibernate, a de facto standard in the software industry, provides the basis for the object-relational mapping (ORM) in Grails. The Spring Framework supplies the core of the Grails Model-View-Controller (MVC) architecture and enables powerful dependency injection. SiteMesh brings flexible and effective layout management to Grails. And, let's not forget Java. Because of Groovy's excellent Java integration, Grails applications not only have direct access to the multitude of Java libraries, but also to the enterprise services (distributed transactions, messaging, etc.) provided by JEE application servers – an absolute necessity for many applications. With this firm footing, Grails stands to legitimize rapid web application development on the Java platform and in the enterprise.

Learning by Example

This book introduces Grails by example. We'll see how to quickly build a Grails application from scratch and how to customize it to meet various needs. We'll explore the essence of each concept we encounter along the way, and for readers that may want to dive deeper into certain topics, we'll include pointers (via endnotes) to supplemental information.

In order to follow along, you'll need a basic knowledge of object-oriented programming and MVC web application development, and you'll certainly benefit from a familiarity with

Java (though you can probably get by without it). We'll also see extensive use of Groovy throughout the examples. While this book doesn't aim to teach Groovy, the examples are such that anyone with some programming background should be able to follow along. If at any point you want to explore a particular Groovy idiom in more detail, be sure to check the Groovy site for further information.[2]

The RaceTrack Application

Over the course of this book, we'll explore the various aspects of Grails development as we build a small web application called *RaceTrack*. There's a regional running club in the southeastern United States that currently uses a paper-based process for tracking the races that the club participates in and the runners that register for each race. They're ready to make the leap into the digital era. For starters, they want an application that will allow the club's staff members to manage the races and registrations. They assure us they don't need anything too fancy – remember, they're using paper now – so, they'll be happy with an application that provides an internal administrative interface to this data. We'll start off with an intranet app that will provide the requested functionality, but we've heard whispers about eventually – if all goes well – letting runners register themselves for races, thus requiring us to expose the application to external users as well.

Developing the *RaceTrack* application will offer a broad, hands-on exposure to Grails. We'll build a web user interface, manage relationships among database tables, apply validation logic, and develop custom queries. As we continue to expand the application, we'll also explore custom tag libraries, Java integration, security, page layout, and the power of dynamic methods. Before we wrap up, we'll be sure to look at several supporting areas as well, including unit testing, logging, and deployment.

By and large, the information and code segments you need to build the application are included within the text of the book.

There's one exception we'll see towards the end, but we'll call that out at that time. Never fear though; all of the source code for the examples is available for you to download.[3] The code bundle includes a complete snapshot of the application's source code as it exists at the end of each chapter.

2

Lacing Up

Installing a JDK

While Grails only requires JDK 1.4, some of the examples we'll see over the next few chapters will take advantage of various JDK 5 features. You'll need JDK 5 in order to work through those examples as shown. (We'll be sure to point out those items that depend on JDK 5 along the way.)

So, while we keep in mind that Grails itself plays nicely with JDK 1.4, take a moment to download and install JDK 5 (http://java.sun.com/javase/downloads/) so you can follow along with these particular examples.[4] Then, set your JAVA_HOME environment variable to point to your JDK 5 installation.

Installing Grails

Next, download the current stable release of Grails from http://grails.org/Download.[5] (This book uses Grails 0.3.1 – the current stable release as of this writing.) Then, follow the quick setup steps (http://grails.org/Installation) to install Grails on your system and configure the necessary environment variables.[6]

Installing a Database

Grails conveniently ships with an embedded copy of HSQLDB, thus giving each Grails app a default in-memory database. That option works great for quick demos and allows you to easily experiment on various features when working side-by-side with a customer. For longer-term needs, we turn to a more traditional

5

disk-based database (which safely preserves our data even when we occasionally restart the application).

While Grails works with most databases (including Oracle, DB2, PostgreSQL, etc.), we'll use MySQL 5.0 for this example. You can download a copy of MySQL Community Edition from http://dev.mysql.com/downloads/mysql/5.0.html, follow the installation instructions, and we'll be ready to go.[7]

3

Hello, Grails!

Creating Your First Grails Application

Now that we have Grails installed, let's create a directory for our Grails applications. You can call it whatever you like, and place it wherever you prefer.

```
jason> mkdir grails_apps
jason> cd grails_apps
grails_apps>
```

Next, from within the directory we just created, let's generate our project structure. Enter grails create-app, and when asked for an application name, enter racetrack.

```
grails_apps> grails create-app
...
create-app:
    [input] Enter application name:
racetrack
...
BUILD SUCCESSFUL
Total time: 4 seconds
```

Just to make sure all is well with our environment, let's start our application. Move into the new directory created for our application, and then enter grails run-app to start the application.

```
grails_apps> cd racetrack
racetrack> grails run-app
...
run-app:watch-context:
```

7

The application is now waiting for our requests. Open your browser to `http://localhost:8080/racetrack/`, and you should see this friendly message welcoming you to Grails.

What's Inside?

We're well on our way. But, before we go too far, let's have a closer look at just what makes up our new application.

Much of Grails's ability to support rapid application development comes from its emphasis on convention over configuration (a key aspect of the "opinionated software" model popularized by Ruby on Rails). The Grails project structure (shown in Figure 3-1 below) relies heavily on convention and establishes a sensible organizational structure for an application's various artifacts.[8]

```
racetrack
    + grails-app
        + conf            Holds    configuration    settings
                          including    data    sources    for
                          development, test, and production
        + controllers     Holds        (obviously       enough)
                          controllers
        + domain          Holds domain classes
        + i18n            Holds            internationalization
                          resource bundles
        + services        Holds  service  classes  (i.e.,  the
                          Grails   equivalent   of   a   local
                          session bean)
        + taglib          Holds tag libraries
        + views           Holds   view   templates   (with   a
                          subdirectory being created to hold
                          the templates for each controller)
            + layouts     Holds  layout  templates  (available
                          to all controllers)
    + grails-tests        Holds unit tests
    + hibernate           Holds      optional      Hibernate
                          configuration files
    + lib                 Holds any custom libraries needed
                          by the application
    + spring              Holds      optional       Spring
                          configuration files
    + src
        + groovy          Holds  Groovy  source  files  (other
                          than    controller,    domain,    or
                          service classes)
        + java            Holds Java source files
    + web-app
        + css             Holds style sheets
        + images          Holds image files
        + js              Holds JavaScript files and third-
                          party libraries (e.g., Prototype,
                          Yahoo, etc.)
        + WEB-INF         Holds          deployment-related
                          configuration files
        + index.jsp       The application's index page
```

Figure 3-1: Application Directory Structure

Establishing Your Domain

Grails treats the domain classes as the central and most important component of the application. It's from the domain classes that we'll drive everything else that we do in the application. (If you've worked with Ruby on Rails, you'll notice that this is a departure from the Rails approach, where Rails derives the domain model from the underlying database schema.)

In order to understand the data we need to capture, we first reviewed the running club's current process. For starters, they showed us the form they use today to track the information for a given race.

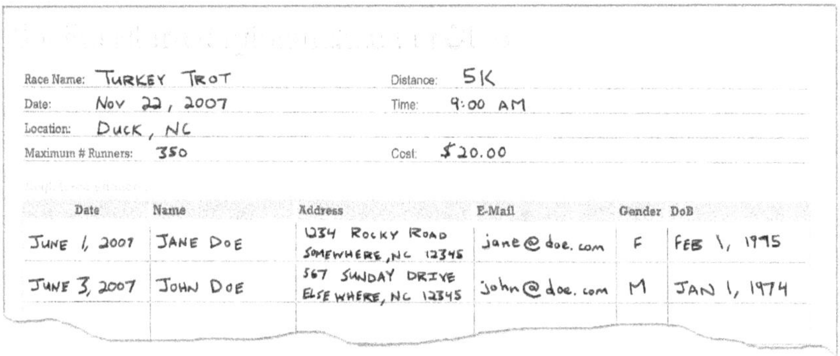

Race Name: TURKEY TROT
Distance: 5K
Date: Nov 22, 2007
Time: 9:00 AM
Location: DUCK, NC
Maximum # Runners: 350
Cost: $20.00

Date	Name	Address	E-Mail	Gender	DoB
JUNE 1, 2007	JANE DOE	1234 ROCKY ROAD SOMEWHERE, NC 12345	jane@doe.com	F	FEB 1, 1975
JUNE 3, 2007	JOHN DOE	567 SUNDAY DRIVE ELSEWHERE, NC 12345	john@doe.com	M	JAN 1, 1974

Figure 3-2: Sample Form Used in Current Paper-Based Process

From this information, we can see that we're basically working with two types of data –races and registrations – and that there's a one-to-many relationship between those entities. That information will form the basis of our domain model, and the various data elements on the form will become the attributes of our domain classes.

So, let's create the domain classes to represent these components. Back in the command prompt, enter `grails create-domain-class`. When prompted for the domain class name, enter `Race`. (If your application is still running from earlier, enter Control-C to stop the application and get back to the command prompt.)

```
racetrack> grails create-domain-class
. . .
create-domain-class:
    [input] Enter domain class name:
Race
. . .
    [echo] Domain class created: grails-app/domain/Race.groovy
. . .
    [echo] Created test suite: grails-tests/RaceTests.groovy
BUILD SUCCESSFUL
Total time: 5 seconds
```

Notice that Grails did not create just the domain class for us, it
also created a corresponding class to hold the unit tests for that
domain class. We'll be sure to make use of that later.

Next, repeat this process to create the `Registration` domain
class.

Now, let's take a look at the domain classes as they exist out-of-
the-box. Open `racetrack/grails-app/domain/Race.groovy`
in your editor of choice.

```
class Race {
}
```

Admittedly, we can't exactly say that we're impressed just yet,
but bear with me for a few minutes. It gets better.

From our earlier discussions with the customer and from
analyzing the paper form, we know the attributes we need to
capture for each race, so let's add those properties to the domain
class.

```
class Race {
    String name
    Date startDateTime
    String city
    String state
    Float distance
    Float cost
    Integer maxRunners = 100000

    static hasMany = [registrations:Registration]
}
```

OK. So, most of that looks pretty straightforward. A race has a name, a starting date/time, etc. Each race will have 100,000 maximum runners by default. That's easy enough, and all the data types look familiar, but what's this hasMany thing all about?

We know from a business standpoint that races and registrations have a one-to-many relationship. Our Race domain model includes the hasMany property to support that relationship. The hasMany property tells Grails that a Race has a one-to-many relationship with some class. To identify the class involved in the relationship, we assign a map of property name – class name pairs to the hasMany property. In this case, we declare that the registrations property will hold a collection of Registration objects.

Notice that we did not explicitly define the registrations property. (This is just a preview of the concise and expressive nature of a Grails application.) Inside the hasMany map, we told Grails that a Race object should store its collection of Registration objects in a property named registrations. Grails therefore knows that we expect a Race object to have this property, so why should we have to declare it again with the other properties? Grails embraces the DRY (Don't Repeat Yourself) principle[9], and spares us from unnecessary redundancy as much as possible.

It's worth noting that, since we declare this information in a map, we're not limited to a single one-to-many relationship for any given domain class. If, for example, we wanted to keep track of the sponsors for a race, we'd just add another entry to the map.

```
static hasMany = [ registrations : Registration,
                   sponsors : Sponsor ]
```

Of course, one-to-many isn't the only relationship type you're likely to encounter. Grails also supports one-to-one, many-to-one, and many-to-many relationships as well.[10]

On to the other side of the relationship. Point your editor at `racetrack/grails-app/ domain/Registration.groovy` and let's define its properties.

```
class Registration {
    Race race
    String name
    Date dateOfBirth
    String gender = 'F'
    String postalAddress
    String emailAddress
    Date createdAt = new Date()
    static belongsTo = Race
    static optionals = ["postalAddress" ]
}
```

Once again, most of these attributes look fairly normal: name, date of birth, etc. There are just a few we need to look at more closely.

Our business users have told us that all of the race attributes are mandatory, and most registration attributes are mandatory as well. However, the users seem to think that this Internet thing is going to catch on, so they've decided that an e-mail address is sufficient, and that the postal address should be an optional property. You'll notice that we haven't stated anywhere in the code that certain fields are mandatory. That's because Grails, by default, assumes that a field is indeed mandatory. If a particular field is not mandatory, then we need to declare it as such. To do so, we define the `optionals` property, which, plainly enough, declares a list of properties that are optional for the domain class. If we wanted to define another property, such as gender, as optional, we'd just include it in the list as well.

```
static optionals = ["postalAddress", "gender" ]
```

In the `Race` domain class, we declared that a `Race` object will hold zero or more `Registration` objects. You'll notice that we didn't explicitly say anywhere whether a `Registration` object can exist on its own (i.e., without a corresponding `Race` object). We obviously know that you cannot register for something that does not exist, so how do we tell Grails that a registration is dependent upon a race? Well, since we now know that all fields are mandatory by default, we can see that we won't be able to save a `Registration` object unless it has a non-null value for its `race` property. So, in essence, we have indeed declared that a `Registration` object cannot exist on its own.

The `belongsTo` property identifies the owning side of the one-to-many relationship between races and registrations. Because we declare that a registration belongs to a race (identified by the registration's `race` property), Grails will ensure that deleting a registration will not delete the corresponding race; however, deleting a race will in fact delete all associated registrations.

Familiar Territory

Now that we've seen the domain model, we can see that Grails very much embraces object-oriented programming. We'd likely model these components in a similar manner in Java or Ruby or any other object-oriented language. In fact, as we move forward, you'll find that the OO and MVC concepts you've come to know and love will continue to serve you well with Grails.

Where's the Beef?

Before we move on to the controllers, notice for a moment that there's nothing in these classes that mentions any kind of Object Relational Mapping (ORM) or persistence. These classes don't seem to extend any other classes that provide that functionality. They don't implement any interface that might identify these classes as needing persistence. Neither do they include any associations to classes that might provide persistence services. And, we didn't edit any configuration files. What tells Grails that these classes need persistence support?

Convention removes the need for any of these approaches. By convention, Grails automatically recognizes the classes in `racetrack/grails-app/domain` as domain classes, and Grails knows that domain classes need persistence. Simply by following this convention, Grails handles all the persistence work for us, thus freeing us up to work on the more difficult and interesting problems.

In the background, Grails Object Relational Mapping (GORM) steps in to provide the necessary persistence functionality. GORM does all the heavy lifting when it comes to persistence logic for a Grails application. (Under the hood, GORM currently relies on Hibernate, but it will offer JPA support as well in an upcoming release.)

Taking Control

Now we're ready for the real time savings to begin. There is just no escaping most of the things we've done so far. (No matter how smart your framework is, you'll always have to describe what data you need to manage.) However, building a good and functional starting point for your user interface is no longer a manual task. It's time to add the controllers.

Make sure you're in the project's root directory – in our case, it's racetrack. Then, enter grails create-controller, and tell Grails to create a controller for the Race domain class.

```
racetrack> grails create-controller
...
create-controller:
    [input] Enter controller name:
Race
...
    [echo] Created controller:
       grails-app/controllers/RaceController.groovy
...
BUILD SUCCESSFUL
Total time: 3 seconds
```

Now, let's open up our new controller and see what we have to start with. Find your way to racetrack/grails-app/controllers/RaceController.groovy, and have a look.

```
class RaceController {
    def index = { }
}
```

Hmm. Well, our ultimate goal is to have a user interface for managing race data. So, we need to include logic in the controller to support listing, creating, updating, and deleting race records. Let's add the necessary code to meet these requirements. How many lines of code should that take?

```
class RaceController {
    def scaffold = Race
}
```

What the heck is that?! Well, actually, it's the code to provide the CRUD (Create-Read-Update-Delete) functionality we're after. When Grails sees the scaffold property in a controller, it will *dynamically* generate the controller logic and the necessary views for the specified domain class, all from that one line of code!

Don't just take my word for it, let's repeat this process for the registration data, and then we'll be ready to see the application in action. Follow these same steps to create a RegistrationController class.

```
class RegistrationController {
    def scaffold = Registration
}
```

Now, it's time to see what we've done. From within your application directory (racetrack), enter grails run-app. Once you see the application start successfully, open a browser and navigate to http://localhost:8080/racetrack.

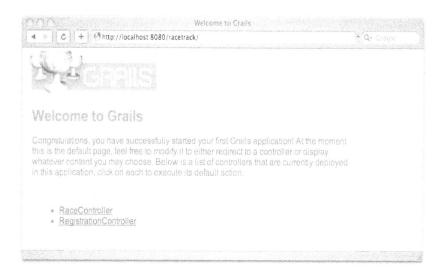

OK. We have our two controllers. And, as is suggested by the text here, we'll eventually want to replace this page with our own custom landing page. For now, let's move on to the `RaceController`.

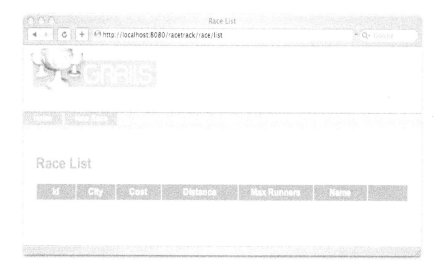

We see most of the columns we'd expect here, but it's not particularly exciting without any data. Click on *New Race* to create some data to work with, and then spend some time exploring the application as it exists so far. Once you add a few records, go back and edit an existing race, delete a race, and try out similar features for managing registrations. Along the way, make note of the things you'd *want* to change as well as the things we *need* to change. At the same time, be sure to consider those things that already meet your needs. Those are the features you got for free!

You likely noticed that a handful of areas obviously need some work, but otherwise, much of the application can probably be ready to go with just a few cosmetic changes.

Here's my take on the list of things we need, and then we'll be sure to cover those nice-to-have items later.

- Validation – We never told Grails that a race must have a distance greater than zero, that a race name shouldn't exceed fifty characters, or that "squirrel" is not a valid gender. So, validation is simply absent, but we can quickly add it.
- Field/Column Ordering – When we're viewing race data, why is the city shown first and the state shown last with

other fields appearing in between? Well, we never told Grails otherwise. The solution to this problem is pleasantly simple, as we'll see in a moment.

- Record Identifiers – When we're editing an individual registration, take a look at what gets shown in the *Race* field. Can you remember which race is "Race: 1" and which is "Race: 2?" A similar issue exists when editing an individual race and viewing its registrations. We'll want to add a bit more clarity to this data.

That's it. If we can tackle these few items, we will have a fully-functioning web app to manage our race and registration data. After that, the rest is just gravy. (Though we'll be sure to have a large helping of that tasty gravy before we're finished.)

Where's My Data?

Isn't there something else we need to handle first? We never told Grails anything about the MySQL database we installed. That in-memory database is indeed handy at times, especially for initial experimentation. But, when we restart the application, we'll lose all the data we just entered. That's okay for now, but as we go forward, we surely don't want to spend all our time reentering test data. So, now that we're happy with our initial domain model, let's ask Grails to start using our MySQL database to back our application.

Quick Note: If we were simply trying to avoid reentering test data, we could consider using Grails bootstrap classes to help us out here, and then we could stick with the in-memory database a while longer. Bootstrap classes provide a handy mechanism for performing various initialization tasks, including populating database tables. However, bootstrap classes will always reinitialize the application with the same data, and we'll lose any data changes we've made whenever we restart the application. So, we'll opt instead for hooking up a traditional database, and we'll cover bootstrap classes later on in Chapter 6.

If you look in `racetrack/grails-app/conf/`, you'll notice that our application includes a data source configuration file for each of the common environments: development, test, and production. We'll want to create a separate database for each of these environments:

- Development – We'll define a database named `racetrack_dev` to support our development efforts, and we'll place the corresponding configuration settings in `racetrack/grails-app/conf/DevelopmentDataSource.groovy`.
- Test – Our unit and functional tests will rely on the `racetrack_test` database to be referenced in `racetrack/grails-app/conf/TestDataSource.groovy`.
- Production – Lastly we'll create a `racetrack_prod` database. With the help of `racetrack/grails-app/conf/ProductionDataSource.groovy`, we'll use this environment to share our application with the world and become billionaires overnight!

So let's get to it…

Back in the command prompt, follow the steps below to create the necessary databases and grant the appropriate access privileges. (I've opted to use my personal user ID for the development and test environments and an alternate top-secret user ID and password for production. Feel free to do as you see fit.)

```
racetrack> mysql -u root -p
Enter password: ********
Welcome to the MySQL monitor.  Commands end with ; or \g.
...
mysql> create database racetrack_dev;
...
mysql> create database racetrack_test;
...
mysql> create database racetrack_prod;
...
mysql> grant all on racetrack_dev.* to
'jason'@'localhost' identified by '';
...
```

```
mysql> grant all on racetrack_test.* to
'jason'@'localhost' identified by '';
...
mysql> grant all on racetrack_prod.* to
'prod'@'localhost' identified by 'wahoowa';
...
mysql> exit
```

Now we're ready to tell Grails about these databases. Open `DevelopmentDataSource.groovy` in your editor and modify it to match the settings below. You'll find this file in `racetrack/grails-app/conf/`. (Note that you'll need to change the `username` and `password` to the appropriate values for your MySQL account.)

```
class DevelopmentDataSource {
    boolean pooling = true
    String dbCreate = "update"
    String url = "jdbc:mysql://localhost/racetrack_dev"
    String driverClassName = "com.mysql.jdbc.Driver"
    String username = "jason"
    String password = ""
}
```

Note that we changed the value of the `dbCreate` property to `"update"`. This value instructs Grails to alter your database schema at runtime to synchronize it with your domain classes, whenever the two do not match. Because we don't have any tables at all yet, Grails will create the tables for our domain classes the next time we start the application. Allowing Grails to handle the database schema for us is yet another rapid application development feature to boost our productivity.

Of course, there will be times when the database already exists, or we just want to manage the database ourselves. Grails supports that approach as well. By simply removing the `dbCreate` property altogether, Grails will leave the database schema unaltered.

We'll come back to configure the test and production data sources later, once we get closer to those stages of our development.

We've almost got the application wired to our database now. We told Grails the class name for the database driver we want to use. Now we just need to supply that driver. Download the Java MySQL driver from http://www.mysql.com/products/connector/j/. I opted for the current production-ready version which, as of this writing, is 5.0.4.[11]

Open the zip file and extract the `mysql-connector-java-5.0.4-bin.jar` file into the `lib` directory of your Grails application – in our case, that's `racetrack/lib`. (Please note that the exact name of the JAR file may differ based on the version of the driver you downloaded.)

Now we're ready to start the app and see our more persistent application in action. (If your application is still running from earlier, enter `Control-C` to stop the application and get back to the command prompt.)

```
racetrack> grails run-app
...
run-app:watch-context:
```

You can try out the application again if you like, but on the surface, nothing should have changed. It's the back end that we're interested in at the moment. Let's go have a look at our development database. We should see one table for each of our domain classes.

```
racetrack> mysql
Welcome to the MySQL monitor.  Commands end with ; or \g.
...
mysql> use racetrack_dev
...
Database changed
mysql> show tables;
+-----------------------+
| Tables_in_racetrack_dev |
+-----------------------+
| race                  |
| registration          |
+-----------------------+
2 rows in set (0.00 sec)
```

```
mysql> describe race;
+-----------------+--------------+------+-----+---------+----------------+
| Field           | Type         |Null |Key |Default | Extra          |
+-----------------+--------------+------+-----+---------+----------------+
|id               | bigint(20)   | NO  |PRI | NULL    | auto_increment |
|version          | bigint(20)   | NO  |    |         |                |
|distance         | float        | NO  |    |         |                |
|max_runners      | int(11)      | NO  |    |         |                |
|start_date_time  | datetime     | NO  |    |         |                |
|state            | varchar(255) | NO  |    |         |                |
|cost             | float        | NO  |    |         |                |
|name             | varchar(255) | NO  |    |         |                |
|city             | varchar(255) | NO  |    |         |                |
+-----------------+--------------+------+-----+---------+----------------+
9 rows in set (0.00 sec)

mysql> describe registration;
+-----------------+--------------+------+-----+---------+----------------+
| Field           | Type         |Null |Key |Default | Extra          |
+-----------------+--------------+------+-----+---------+----------------+
|id               | bigint(20)   | NO  |PRI | NULL    | auto_increment |
|version          | bigint(20)   | NO  |    |         |                |
|gender           | varchar(255) | NO  |    |         |                |
|date_of_birth    | datetime     | NO  |    |         |                |
|postal_address   | varchar(255) | YES |    | NULL    |                |
|email_address    | varchar(255) | NO  |    |         |                |
|created_at       | datetime     | NO  |    |         |                |
|race_id          | bigint(20)   | YES |MUL | NULL    |                |
|name             | varchar(255) | NO  |    |         |                |
+-----------------+--------------+------+-----+---------+----------------+
9 rows in set (0.00 sec)

mysql>
```

Let's take a moment to discuss the schema Grails generated for us. This is another area where conventions play an important role in Grails. Notice that...

- The table names exactly match the domain class names.
- The column names match the class's property names.
- For multi-word property names, the column separates the words with an underscore (e.g., the property maxRunners maps to the max_runners column).
- The id column is used as the primary key for each table and it's defined as an auto_increment column, thus allowing Grails to rely on the database to auto-generate unique IDs for new records.
- For one-to-many relationships, the child table will include a column to hold the ID of the parent record. The column is named using the name of the parent

domain class – in this case, Race – and declares a foreign key constraint referring back to the parent table. Here, this results in the race_id column.

You may be wondering why we see the id and version columns here, but we didn't see any corresponding properties in our domain classes. Since every Grails domain class needs these properties, GORM injects them into the class for us at compile time. We don't need to explicitly declare them. (In case you're wondering, the version property is used by Hibernate to support transaction management and optimistic locking. It's important that it exists, but beyond that, we can safely ignore this attribute.)

As a side note, many database administrators will no doubt cringe at the thought of defining a VARCHAR(255) column for a field that will never exceed 50 characters or a DATETIME column for a field that only needs to hold a date and no time data. So, some folks will inevitably want to create and manage their tables on their own (instead of having Grails do so). If you take this approach and make sure your schema still follows the conventions mentioned above, Grails will automatically know how to map your domain classes to your database. If you have to deviate from these conventions, you're not out of luck, but you'll need to provide some configuration information to tell Grails how to perform the proper mapping.

That gives us an overview of the key database conventions used in Grails. We'll cover these topics in more detail in chapter 9. In the mean time, now that we have a database that will preserve our data across restarts, let's get back to the application improvements we identified earlier.

Building Better Scaffolding

For starters, we mentioned that we need validation and better field ordering. Grails provides a way for us to satisfy both of these needs in one easy step.

Declaring Constraints

Grails constraints declare our expectations for the property values of a domain class. We use constraints to declare that a particular property cannot exceed a certain length, that a property has a finite list of valid values, that a property must hold a syntactically-valid e-mail address, and so on.[12] We define the constraints using a Groovy closure[13] in the domain class, and the closure uses the handy Groovy builder syntax[14] to easily and clearly define the constraints.

Let's start with `Race` domain class. Add the closure shown below to `Race.groovy`.

```
class Race {
    //...
    static constraints = {
        name(maxLength:50,blank:false)
        startDateTime(min:new Date())
        city(maxLength:30,blank:false)
        state(inList:['GA', 'NC', 'SC', 'VA'],blank:false)
        distance(min:3.1f,max:100f)
        cost(min:0f,max:999.99f)
    }
}
```

This mechanism reads so cleanly and intuitively that it needs almost no explanation. For example, we can plainly see that the `name` property has a maximum length of fifty characters and that it cannot be blank.

Perhaps you're thinking, "But didn't we already say that the `name` property is mandatory?" You're correct. Grails will throw an exception if any mandatory properties are null when persisting a domain object to the database. But we'd prefer a more graceful way to handle any such issues, and we'd also like to make sure we have a valid object before we ever get to the persistence tier. The constraints satisfy that need. When calling the `validate` or `save` method on a domain object, Grails checks the object against the defined constraints and reports back any issues.[15] Grails will not persist the object to the database if it fails to satisfy the constraints.

Let's quickly run down the other constraints in the order they appear above.

- The race cannot start in the past.
- The city property has a maximum length of thirty characters, and it cannot be blank.
- The state must be one of the four states in the list – since it's a regional club – and it cannot be blank.
- The distance must be between 3.1 miles (5 km) and 100 miles (160.9 km).
- The cost must be between $0 and $999.99.

Wait a second. There's something not quite right about our constraint for the startDateTime property. Our business rule states – and common sense agrees – that a race cannot start in the past, but as it stands now, the minimum date/time will get set when this class is initialized. That means, after the application has been running for a few days, users can indeed create races that supposedly start in the past, just so long as the starting date/time is sometime *after* we started the application. That's clearly not the desired functionality. We need the constraint to compare the given value to the *current* date/time. Fortunately, Grails allows us to define custom validators to meet the special needs of our application.[16] In this case, let's replace the startDateTime constraint above with the following declaration.

```
startDateTime(validator: {return (it > new Date())})
```

Custom validators are defined as closures. This particular validator compares the startDateTime value (represented by the it variable) to the current date/time and returns the Boolean result. If the value is valid, then the validator (obviously) won't return any errors. On the other hand, if the closure returns false, then the constraint will generate a validation error and prevent the object from being persisted.

Ordering UI Fields

While it's not immediately apparent, we've also handled our need to reorder the user interface fields. The fields will now appear in the order defined in the `constraints` closure. If you have a property that doesn't need constraints but should still appear at a certain position in the user interface, you can still include that property in the `constraints` closure. For example, if we wanted the `maxRunners` property to appear as the first field, we could have included it as the first item in the closure with an empty set of rules.

```
static constraints = {
    maxRunners()
    //...
}
```

Now that we understand how constraints work, let's quickly add the constraints for the `Registration` domain class. Add the closure shown below to `Registration.groovy`.

```
class Registration {
    //...
    static constraints = {
        name(maxLength:50,blank:false)
        dateOfBirth(nullable:false)
        gender(inList:["M", "F"])
        postalAddress(maxLength:255)
        emailAddress(maxLength:50,email:true)
        race(nullable:false)
    }
}
```

The next time we restart our application, we'll see that we've now handled both the validation and the field ordering issues.

Meaningful Record Identifiers

When viewing the details for an individual race, we mentioned that we'd like a more meaningful way to represent a registration than "Registration: 1," "Registration: 4," etc. And we want to add similar clarity for identifying races. (If every problem were this easy to solve, we'd all be on the golf course by 9:30 a.m.

every day – a full half hour early.) The solution is as simple as overriding the default `toString` method for each domain class. We'll start by adding the method to `Race.groovy`.

```
class Race {
    //...
    String toString() {"${this.name} : ${this.city},
                        ${this.state}" }
}
```

If you're new to Groovy, you'll quickly come to appreciate Groovy GStrings.[17] GStrings allow you to embed an expression into a String to be evaluated at runtime. It's certainly not revolutionary, but it's a welcome alternative to Java string concatenation or StringBuffers. This particular method will return values such as "Turkey Trot : Duck, NC." That certainly offers more clarity than "Race: 1"!

That was easy enough. Let's clear things up in `Registration.groovy` as well. The name and e-mail address should serve well to identify a registrant.

```
class Registration {
    //...
    String toString(){"${this.name}:${this.emailAddress}"}
}
```

The Results Are In

Ready to see the fruits of our labor? At the command line, enter `grails run-app`. Wait to see the application start successfully, and then open your browser to http://localhost:8080/racetrack.

Let's first have a look at the race list, and observe the vastly improved column ordering.

Did you notice that the list doesn't show the maximum runners for each race? That's because the default scaffolding list view will only show up to six properties. If you have constraints defined, it will show the `id` property and then the first five properties listed in the constraints closure. Grails clearly had to draw the line somewhere, and this behavior tends to yield a reasonably-sized table and prevent dreaded horizontal scrolling.

We should also note that the scaffolding is intended to serve as a helpful starting point for our application, to be customized as we see fit. So, if you want additional columns, you can certainly add them. But hold that thought; we'll soon see how to make rather significant changes to the user interface.

Let's try out the validation, shall we? It's always fun to try to break an application, so have at it.

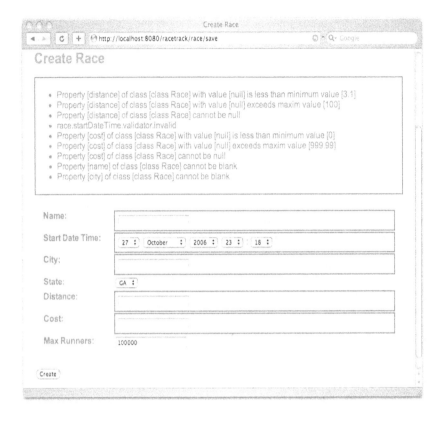

When we try to create an invalid race, we don't just get error messages, we also get some fairly nice visual cues indicating the problematic fields. Naturally we'll want change the error messages to something more business-focused and less technical, and we'll handle that shortly. In the meantime, it's nice to know that the system is protected against bogus data.

The scaffolding has also generated a few other improvements based on our constraints. Notice that the UI now renders a select box (instead of a generic text field) for the state property. Also, the form fields now limit the amount of text you can enter for the properties that have maximum length constraints (e.g., name, city, etc.). So, we now have both client-side enforcement (via the HTML form elements) and server-side enforcement (via the domain class).

Lastly, let's check out the record identifier improvements.

Much better! We can clearly see now that Jane Doe and John Doe have registered for this race. That's quite a bit more usable than the mysterious integers previously displayed here.

Let's See the Code!

So far, we've relied on declarative scaffolding, by including the `def scaffold = Race` and `def scaffold = Registration` directives in our controllers. That approach has served us well up to this point, but now we're ready to start customizing the scaffolding.

We could just add new actions to the controllers as they currently exist. Because declarative scaffolding dynamically generates the controller logic, any new actions we define would simply take precedence over the default actions (assuming the name of our new action matches the name of a default action). However, we'll want to make just a *few* tweaks to the existing controller logic over the next few chapters. We can be more productive by generating the scaffolding code and customizing it to meet our needs. To do that, we need access to the real code. So, it's time to *generate* the actual scaffolding logic.

We want to *replace* the existing controllers (and their whopping three lines of code) with controllers that include the scaffolding code. First things first, let's delete the existing controller classes – `RaceController.groovy` and `RegistrationController.groovy`.

Next, make sure you're in the project's root directory – in our case, it's `racetrack`. Then, enter `grails generate-all`. When asked for the domain class name, enter `Race`.

```
racetrack> grails generate-all
...
input-domain-class:
    [input] Enter domain class name:
Race
...
BUILD SUCCESSFUL
Total time: 11 seconds
```

Repeat this process to generate the controller and views for the `Registration` domain class. Now we have full access to the code, and we can customize it as we see fit.

Understanding URLs and Controllers

Now that we can inspect the code, let's take a moment to look at how Grails determines which controller and which action to invoke for a given URL. (Hint: It doesn't involve even a single XML configuration file!)

URL Conventions

Consider the types of URLs we saw as we worked our way through the application:

http://localhost:8080/racetrack/race/
http://localhost:8080/racetrack/race/create
http://localhost:8080/racetrack/registration/show/2

Each component of the URL plays an important role in the Grails convention. And it's by following that convention that we (thankfully) free ourselves from having to wire together our URLs, controllers, and views in external configuration files.

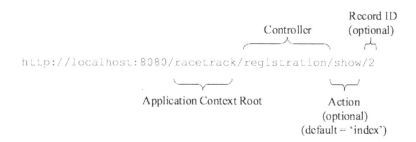

Figure 3-3: URL Structure

The first component is the application context root, which of course, identifies the name of the application as it was registered with the server. (By default, Grails uses the application name as the context root and automatically registers the application with the server when we invoke grails run-app.)

The next component is used to identify the controller that will handle the request. Given a URL where this component is "registration", Grails will attempt to route the request to a controller named "RegistrationController". (If no such controller exists, we can expect to see a trusty HTTP 404 error.)

Grails then looks for a component specifying the action to invoke within the given controller. If the URL includes the action, then Grails will invoke that action in the controller. (Again, if the action does not exist, we'll get an error.) If the URL does not include an action, Grails invokes the default action for the controller. Unless otherwise specified in the controller, Grails looks for an action named "index" as the default action.[18]

Lastly, Grails looks for a component specifying the ID for a particular record. If such a component is present in the URL, Grails adds a parameter named "id" to the request with this value. In the example above, the "id" parameter would have a value of "2".

From Request to Controller to View

Let's look at a few code examples from `RaceController.groovy`, and walk through what happens when Grails receives a request for http://localhost:8080/racetrack/race/.

First, because no action is specified, Grails routes the request to the `index` action. (Note that all actions are implemented as Groovy closures.)

```
def index = {
    redirect(action:list,params:params)
}
```

The default implementation of the `index` action redirects the request to the `list` action. The `redirect` method is just one of many dynamic methods available in Grails controllers.[19]

```
def list = {
    if (!params.max) params.max = 10
    [ raceList: Race.list( params ) ]
}
```

The `list` action also includes a pleasantly concise implement-tation. The first statement supports the built-in pagination funct-ionality that, by default, displays a maximum of ten records per page. The second statement is what really matters here. It declares and returns a map with a single key (`raceList`) whose value is the list of `Race` objects for all races in the database. (For now, know that the `list` method is one of the many dynamic methods provided for domain classes.[20] We'll explore these methods in more detail shortly.)

We're finished with the controller, but once this action returns, what component renders the actual view that we see in the browser? Well, it's convention (once again) that allows the `list` method to be so concise. Because we're inside

RaceController and returning from the list action, Grails knows to use the view template located at racetrack/grails-app/views/race/list.gsp.

Grails uses GSPs (Groovy Server Pages) to provide the templates for the views. If you've used JSPs (JavaServer Pages), you'll recognize the familiar syntax. As the name suggests, the main difference between GSPs and JSPs is the use of Groovy instead of Java to provide scriptlets. As you'll see, Groovy kindly cuts down the amount of code we need to write in order to get our point across.

Now, let's explore list.gsp for a moment. If we look at part of the template, we can see that it uses the raceList variable (returned by the list method) to render the response.

```
<g:each in="${raceList}">
    <tr>
        <td>${it.id}</td>
        <td>${it.name}</td>
        <td>${it.startDateTime}</td>
        <td>${it.city}</td>
        <td>${it.state}</td>
        <td>${it.distance}</td>
        <td class="actionButtons">
            <span class="actionButton">
                <g:link action="show" id="${it.id}">
                        Show
                </g:link>
            </span>
        </td>
    </tr>
</g:each>
```

In this example, the <g:each> tag iterates over the list and renders the tag body once for each object in the list. In each iteration, the tag body can access the current list item using the it variable. For example, it.name returns the value of the name property for the current Race object.

Of course, you won't always have a one-to-one mapping between actions and view templates. So, when no view template exists that matches the action name (or you just don't want to use that template), Grails allows you to explicitly specify the view template to be used. The save method (in RaceController.groovy) includes an example of this approach.

```
def save = {
    def race = new Race()
    race.properties = params
    if(race.save()) {
        redirect(action:show,id:race.id)
    }
    else {
        render(view:'create',model:[race:race])
    }
}
```

Here, if the race.save() call returns false, the action instructs Grails to render the create template (racetrack/grails-app/views/race/create.gsp) using the race object to populate the form.

Controller Lifecycle

Before we leave this topic, we should quickly mention the lifecycle of a Grails controller. It's worth noting that Grails creates a new controller instance for each request, and the controller only lives long enough to process that request. So, if you absolutely must, you can safely add instance variables to your controllers without any multi-user threading concerns. Just remember that you probably don't want to try this in any of the traditional Java-based MVC frameworks you might be used to using.

4

Improving the User Experience

At this point, we've developed an application that meets our needs, but it could still use some polish to make it a bit more user friendly. And since we want our users to enjoy our application, let's spend some time adding in some of those nice-to-have items.

- Error Messages – We noted that the validation error messages could use some work, so we should customize them to be less technical and more meaningful to the end-user.
- Warning and Confirmation Messages – Did you try to delete any records? Were you surprised when the application deleted the record without asking you for any kind of confirmation? Most users would expect a warning before deleting a record, so we'll add that feature. We'll also add logic to display confirmation messages *after* we add, update, or delete a record.
- Record IDs – While the database and the application rely heavily on record IDs, end users don't tend to have much use for them. End users want to see the business data (e.g., race name, registration date/time, etc.), and we really shouldn't concern them with underlying implementation details like record IDs.
- Data Formatting – A truly professional application displays its data in the appropriate format. We have some work to do in this area. For example, the *Date of Birth* field on the registration page really shouldn't include the time of day. It's just not relevant. The

various numeric and currency values could benefit from improved formatting as well.

Customizing Error Messages

Each validation constraint has a pre-defined list of error codes it can return. So far, we've seen only the default text for those error messages. As we start to define custom error messages, we'll want to refer to the Grails reference documentation to determine the message code(s) associated with each constraint.[12]

For starters, let's look at the error message that accompanies a blank race name.

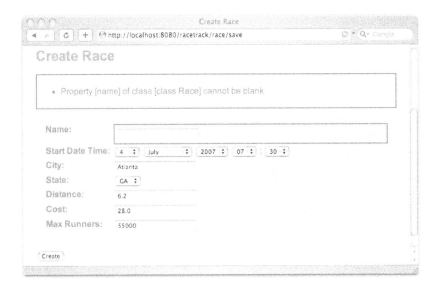

We need to review the domain class to find the name of the constraints we applied to the race name property.

```
static constraints = {
    name(maxLength:50,blank:false)
    //...
}
```

The name of the constraint to check for blank values is, plainly enough, "blank." We can now look up that constraint in the Grails reference documentation.

The documentation tells us that this constraint generates an error code with the following naming convention.

```
className.propertyName.blank
```

So, to customize the error message, we want to add an entry with this pattern to racetrack/grails-app/i18n/messages.properties.

```
race.name.blank=Please enter a name for this race
```

Once we've added this entry, let's restart the application and try it out.

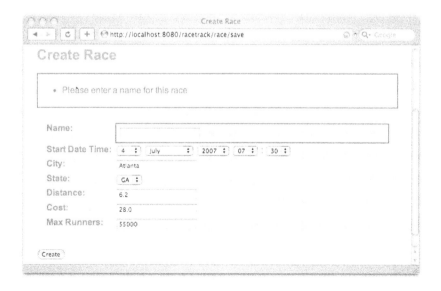

For some constraints, Grails also supplies runtime arguments that you can include in your messages. You can look at the default error messages (in `messages.properties`) to help you determine the value provided in each argument. For example, the `max` constraint's error message includes an argument specifying the maximum allowable value. That information will go a long way towards improving our application's usability, and we'd certainly rather not duplicate that value in `messages.properties` when it already exists in the constraint itself (in `Race.groovy`). From examining the default error message for this constraint (defined as `default.invalid.max.length.message`), we can determine that the message's fourth argument indicates the maximum value. (Because the argument array uses a zero-based index, we access the fourth argument using an index of 3.)

```
Property [{0}] of class [{1}] with value [{2}] exceeds
the maximum length of [{3}]
```

So, we can define the following entry in `messages.properties` to provide the desired error text for a race distance that exceeds the maximum allowable value.

```
race.distance.max.exceeded=Please enter a valid distance
no more than {3} miles
```

And we now have an error message that provides all the information the user needs in order to address the problem.

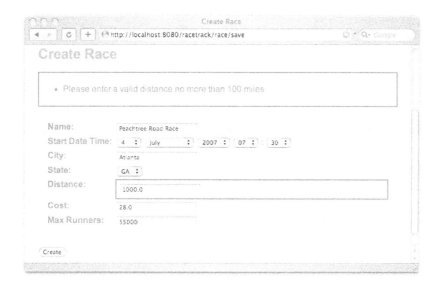

Now that we know how to customize an error message, we just repeat the process for the remaining constraints. (Of course, you'll probably want to customize several messages at a time, unless you *really* enjoy restarting your server.)

Adding Warning Messages

Without a doubt, users expect an application to warn them before performing any destructive actions. Deleting data certainly qualifies as destructive activity, especially when you consider that deleting a race also deletes all the corresponding registrations. So, let's add some logic to get the user's approval before deleting any records.

Because a user can delete a race from either the *Show Race* page or the *Edit Race* page, we'll want to define our warning logic in a common place for use by both pages. We'll use a JavaScript dialog to provide the warning message, so let's create a file (`racetrack/web-app/js/racetrack.js`) to hold the common JavaScript functions for the application. Add the following function to `racetrack.js`.

```
function warnBeforeRaceDelete() {
    return confirm('Are you sure you want to delete this race?')
}
```

Now we need to call this function from the *Show Race* and *Edit Race* pages. Open the template for the *Show Race* page (`racetrack/grails-app/views/race/show.gsp`), and add the `script` tag shown below, which allows this page to reference the functions in `racetrack.js`.

```
<head>
<meta http-equiv="Content-Type" content="text/html;
charset=UTF-8"/>
    <g:javascript library="racetrack" />
    <meta name="layout" content="main" />
    <title>Show Race</title>
</head>
```

Then, find the *Delete* button and add the `onclick` attribute shown below to call our new function. If the user chooses to delete the race, the function will return `true`, the browser will submit the form, and the application will delete the race. Otherwise, the function will return `false`, and the browser won't submit the form.

```
<g:form controller="race">
    <input type="hidden" name="id" value="${race?.id}" />
    <span class="button">
        <g:actionSubmit value="Edit"/>
    </span>
    <span class="button">
        <g:actionSubmit value="Delete"
                        onclick="return
                        warnBeforeRaceDelete();"
        />
    </span>
</g:form>
```

Now let's try to delete a race from the *Show Race* page.

That's just what we wanted. It's simple, but important. Go ahead and modify the *Edit Race* page to call this JavaScript function as well. Then, add a similar function to provide a warning before deleting a registration, and call that function from the *Show Registration* and *Edit Registration* pages.

Implementing Confirmation Messages

Confirmation messages are a rather simple feature, but if you've ever used an application that doesn't provide them, you can't help but wonder sometimes if the application has actually done what you've asked. Technically, the user can see the results of her actions as the application exists now. When the user updates a race, the application displays the *Show Race* page with the updated data. But, the user is left to scan the data to make sure her updates are intact. A simple confirmation message should boost the user's confidence in our application.

You may have noticed that the application already displays confirmation messages when we delete a record. We'll piggyback on that existing logic to add confirmation messages after creating or updating a record.

Upon creating or updating a race, the application displays the *Show Race* page. If you look in the template for this page (`racetrack/grails-app/views/race/show.gsp`), you'll see that it already includes logic for displaying confirmation messages (or any other kind of message we deem appropriate).

```
<g:if test="${flash.message}">
    <div class="message">${flash.message}</div>
</g:if>
```

Let's look at the controller logic that supplies the messages, and then we'll discuss just exactly what the code above is all about. Open `RaceController.groovy` and locate the `update` action. Add the logic shown below to assign the confirmation message to `flash.message` when we successfully save a race. (Towards the end of this closure, you'll notice another use of `flash.message` already provided by the default scaffolding.)

```
def update = {
    def race = Race.get( params.id )
    if(race) {
        race.properties = params
        if(race.save()) {
            flash.message = "${params.name} updated."
            redirect(action:show,id:race.id)
        }
        else {
            render(view:'edit',model:[race:race])
        }
    }
    else {
        flash.message = "Race not found with id
                          ${params.id}"
        redirect(action:edit,id:params.id)
    }
}
```

So where does `flash.message` come from? Grails includes the concept of "flash" scope. In the same way that controllers and view templates have access to the request and the session, they also have access to flash scope. And just like request and session parameters, the `flash` object is simply a map of key-value pairs. What makes the flash scope unique is its duration. Items stored in flash scope are available for the duration of the current request *and* the next request. In the example above, we redirect to the *Show Race* page. The redirect generates a new request. If we had stored the message in the request, we would no longer have access to it when we display the *Show Race* page. By using flash scope, we still have access to the message even after the redirect. And upon the end of the second request, Grails then clears the items from flash scope. No manual cleanup necessary.

Let's find a race to update and see if we feel more confident given our new confirmation message.

Looks good. Now let's add logic in the `save` action to display a similar message after creating a new race.

```
def save = {
    def race = new Race()
    race.properties = params
    if(race.save()) {
        flash.message = "${params.name} saved."
        redirect(action:show,id:race.id)
    }
    else {
        render(view:'create',model:[race:race])
    }
}
```

Give this new message a try, and then we'll be finished adding confirmation messages for the race components. Take a moment to add similar confirmation messages for the registration components, and then we're ready for our next task.

Removing Record IDs

Occasionally, you can actually make an application better by removing certain features. Record IDs tend to fall into this category. Our end users just aren't concerned with them, and that's reason enough to remove them from the user interface. Let's start with the *Race List* page. Find the section below in `racetrack/grails-app/views/race/list.gsp,` and remove the ID column.

```
<tr>
    <th>Id</th>
    <th>Name</th>
    <th>Start Date Time</th>
    <th>City</th>
    <th>State</th>
    <th>Distance</th>
    <th></th>
</tr>
<g:each in="${raceList}">
    <tr>
        <td>${it.id}</td>
        <td>${it.name}</td>
        <td>${it.startDateTime}</td>
        <td>${it.city}</td>
        <td>${it.state}</td>
        <td>${it.distance}</td>
        <td class="actionButtons">
            <span class="actionButton">
                <g:link action="show" id="${it.id}">
                    Show
                </g:link>
            </span>
        </td>
    </tr>
</g:each>
```

Now, when we view the *Race List* page, we see only the data that matters to our users.

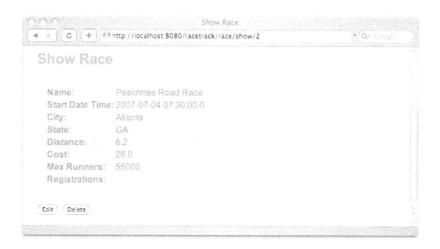

Record IDs also appear on the *Show Race* page, the *Edit Race* page, and the analogous pages for managing registrations. We'll want to track down and remove the IDs from those pages as well.

Formatting Data

There's just no denying that the application could benefit from more appropriate data formatting. We needn't look any further than the *Show Race* page to find an awkwardly formatted date/time value, a monetary value with the wrong precision and no currency symbol, and a few more opportunities for improvement as well.

Apart from assigning a style to the table cells, the application currently uses each property's default `toString` method to render its output.

```
<tr class="prop">
    <td valign="top" class="name">Start Date/Time:</td>
    <td valign="top" class="value">${race.startDateTime}</td>
</tr>
```

Instead of relying on the `toString` method, we need a way to specify our desired format for both dates and numeric values. We could embed the formatting logic directly in the view templates, but that would get rather ugly, and we'd end up with a lot of duplicated code. In this situation, we know that a better choice is to implement a custom tag library. And we're in luck, because adding new tags to Grails is a breeze.

Custom Tag Libraries

Let's start with formatting date/time values. If we can think about the tag as a utility method of sorts, we can ask ourselves what parameters we need to provide to the method and what we expect it to return. In this case, we want to provide the `Date` object and a `string` indicating the desired format. (We'll use the formatting syntax defined in `java.text.SimpleDateFormat`.) Then, we want the tag to output the date the given format. Once we implement our new tag and give it a name – `formatDate` sounds appropriate – we can replace the existing markup (shown above) with markup that formats the date using our custom tag.

```
<tr class="prop">
    <td valign="top" class="name">Start Date/Time:</td>
    <td valign="top" class="value">
        <g:formatDate date="${race.startDateTime}"
                      format="yyyy-MMM-dd HH:mm"/>
    </td>
</tr>
```

Now that we have a basic API for our date-formatting tag, let's look at our number-formatting needs. (We'll first determine the API for both tags, and then we'll move on the actually implementing the tag library.) This tag can likely use a similar approach to that of the `formatDate` tag. We have a number and a desired format – this time we'll use the formatting syntax from `java.text.DecimalFormat` – and we want the tag to output the formatted number. That sounds straightforward enough. So, what would the new markup look like for the various numeric values on the *Show Race* page?

```
<tr class="prop">
    <td valign="top" class="name">Distance:</td>
    <td valign="top" class="value">
        <g:formatNumber number="${race.distance}"
                        format="##0.0 mi"/>
    </td>
</tr>
<tr class="prop">
    <td valign="top" class="name">Cost:</td>
    <td valign="top" class="value">
        <g:formatNumber number="${race.cost}"
                        format="\$##0.00"/>
    </td>
</tr>
<tr class="prop">
    <td valign="top" class="name">Max Runners:</td>
    <td valign="top" class="value">
        <g:formatNumber number="${race.maxRunners}"
                        format="###,##0"/>
    </td>
</tr>
```

We have our APIs, and now we're ready to code the tag library. Grails tag libraries are written (not surprisingly) as Groovy classes. Each tag is defined as a closure, and the closure receives a map containing the tag attributes as an argument at runtime.

Let's define a new Groovy class for our application's custom tags. We'll create a new file called `RaceTrackTagLib.groovy` and place it in the `racetrack/grails-app/taglib` directory.

```
class RaceTrackTagLib {
    /**
     * Outputs the given <code>Date</code> object in the
     * specified format.  If the <code>date</code> is not given,
     * then the current date/time is used. If the
     * <code>format</code> option is not given, then the date is
     * output using the default format.
     *
     * e.g.:
     * <g:formatDate date="${myDate}" format="yyyy-MM-dd HH:mm"/>
     *
     * @see java.text.SimpleDateFormat
```

```
    */
  def formatDate = { attrs ->
      def date = attrs.get('date')

      if (!date) {
            date = new Date()
      }

      def format = attrs.get('format')
      if (!format) {
            format = "yyyy-MM-dd HH:mm:ss z"
      }

      out << new java.text.SimpleDateFormat(format).format(date)
  }

  /**
   * Outputs the given number in the specified format.  If no
   * <code>number</code> is given, then zero is used.  If the
   * <code>format</code> option is not given, then the number
   * is output using the default format.
   *
   * e.g.:
   * <g:formatNumber number="${myNumber}" format="###,##0" />
   *
   * @see java.text.DecimalFormat
   */
  def formatNumber = { attrs ->
      def number = attrs.get('number')

      if (!number) {
            number = new Double(0)
      }

      def format = attrs.get('format')
      if (!format) {
            format = "0"
      }

      out << new java.text.DecimalFormat(format)
                          .format((Double)number)

  }
}
```

Lastly, we need to register the TLD (Tag Library Descriptor). Wait a second. Scratch that. Grails doesn't need any TLDs. TLDs represent configuration, but Grails prefers convention instead. Recall that we placed the tag library in racetrack/grails-app/taglib, and that's exactly where Grails will look when it encounters a tag in the view template. Grails will simply find the closures for each tag and execute them. So, that's it. We're ready to test. Let's take a look at our more properly formatted data.

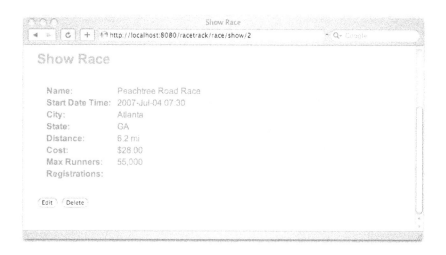

We're making progress. Of course, we should propagate these improvements to the other race pages as well. The *Race List* page can benefit from similar formatting, and the *Create Race* and *Edit Race* pages should include units of measure for the *Distance* field and a currency indicator for the *Cost* field. Once you've made those few enhancements, we'll be ready for our next task.

Standard Tag Libraries

We won't always need a custom tag library to get the job done. Fortunately, Grails offers a healthy serving of standard tags as well.[21] And it's on the registration-related pages that we need to tweak the use of those tags a bit.

Consider the *Create Registration* page for example. This page uses the Grails `datePicker` tag to render the *Date Of Birth* and *Created At* fields. We want the *Created At* field to represent the registration timestamp, and that's something we can determine without user input. In fact, we'd really prefer not to allow the user to edit the field at all; otherwise we could end up with inaccurate data. And as we mentioned before, the time of day is irrelevant when asking for the runner's date of birth.

Back in your editor, open the template for the *Create Registration* page (`racetrack/grails-app/views/registration/create.gsp`). Now, locate the section of the template that renders the *Date Of Birth* field. If we look at the Grails documentation for the `datePicker` tag[22], we see that it supports an optional `precision` parameter. This is exactly what we need. Let's add this parameter to the tag used for the *Date Of Birth* field so that it only renders the year, month, and day.

```
<g:datePicker  name='dateOfBirth'
               value='${registration?.dateOfBirth}'
               precision='day'>
</g:datePicker>
```

That was easy enough. Now, on to our next improvement. Ensuring that we get an accurate registration date is down right trivial – just remove the *Created At* field from the page altogether.

Recall that the `Registration` class initializes the `createdAt` property to the current timestamp. So, when Grails creates a new `Registration` object with the data from the form, the object will already have the correct registration timestamp (i.e., the current date/time).

```
class Registration {
    //...
    Date createdAt = new Date()
    //...
}
```

And now, our slightly-modified page is ready to more accurately capture the data we need.

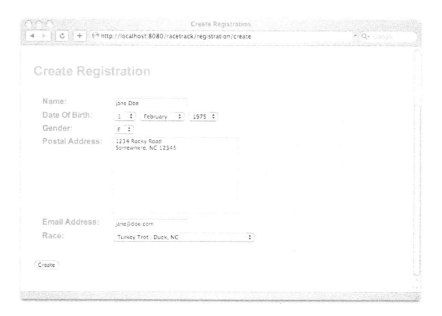

While we're at it, we should also address these fields on the other registration-related pages. We should adjust the precision of the *Date of Birth* field on all pages. On the *Edit Registration* page, we can simply adjust the precision of the `datePicker` tag as we saw above. On the *Registration List and Show Registration* pages, we can use our new `formatDate` tag to show only the month, day, and year.

That leaves us with just the *Created At* field left to handle. We don't ever want to change the value for this field. It represents the time at which the registration was created, and well, you just can't change history. Since the *Edit Registration* page currently allows the user to alter the *Created At* field, we should adjust the page to instead display the field as a read-only value. Take a moment to add that bit of polish to the application, and then we're ready for the next iteration.

5

Get Dynamic

OK. We've worked through a few initial iterations with our users. We've gotten their feedback, and they like what they see so far. They're excited by how quickly we put the application together and how we continue to make small incremental improvements with short turnaround times. Of course, once we have some basic CRUD functionality like this, one of the first requests we get is, "I need a way to find all races scheduled for the month of _____." Or, "Show me all __-mile races located in _____." These are reasonable enough requests, and Grails will help us continue to impress our users as we quickly provide these new reports.

Recall our brief mention of dynamic methods back when we looked the generated controller code? We observed the `list` method – a dynamic method in all domain classes – used to fetch all races for display on the *Race List* page. We didn't have to write any special code in our domain class to obtain that functionality. It simply comes standard with any Grails domain class. As we implement this new query functionality, we'll take a deeper at look at some of the other dynamic methods available for Grails domain classes.

Dynamic Finders

For starters, let's say we need to be able to find all races by city. We'll add a new menu option on the *Race List* page to take us to our new query page. Add this block to the menu section of `racetrack/grails-app/views/race/list.gsp`.

```
<span class="menuButton">
    <g:link action="search">Search for Races</g:link>
</span>
```

Clicking this menu option will invoke a new action in our controller named `search`. For now, we don't need that action to do anything more than render our search input page. So, add an empty closure in `RaceController.groovy` to accept these requests.

```
def search = {
}
```

This empty closure tells Grails that `search` is a valid action for this controller. When Grails receives a request for this action, it will simply look for a template with the same name (i.e., `search.gsp`) in `racetrack/grails-app/views/race/` and render its content.

Since we really just want a simple form with input fields for a race, we can use the `create.gsp` template as a good staring point. When we're finished, our new `search.gsp` template should look like this:

```
<html>
    <head>
        <meta http-equiv="Content-Type" content="text/html;
                charset=UTF-8"/>
        <meta name="layout" content="main" />
        <title>Search for Races</title>
    </head>
    <body>
      <div class="body">
        <h1>Search for Races</h1>
        <g:if test="${flash.message}">
            <div class="message">${flash.message}</div>
        </g:if>
        <g:form action="search" method="post" >
            <div class="dialog">
            <table>
              <tr class='prop'>
                <td valign='top' class='name'>
                    <label for='city'>City:</label>
                </td>
                <td valign='top' class='value'>
                    <input type="text" maxlength='30' name='city'>
                    </input>
                </td>
```

```
            </tr>
          </table>
        </div>
        <div class="buttons">
          <input type="submit" value="Search"
                 class="formbutton">
          </input>
        </div>
      </g:form>
    </div>
  </body>
</html>
```

And now, our new search page awaits.

You'll notice that in `search.gsp` we specified that the form should post all requests to the `search` action.

```
<g:form action="search" method="post" >
```

Our `search` action is currently empty and simply routes to the search input page. Now, we need to add some logic to actually perform the searches.

```
def search = {
    if (request.method == 'POST') {
        render(view:'list', model:[ raceList:
          Race.findAllByCityLike('%' + params.city + '%') ])
    }
}
```

Since we're using the same action to render the search input page and to output the search results, we need a way to determine which function to perform for a given request. We know that the query parameters will arrive in a *post* request, so we'll make sure we only perform a search for *post* requests. For any other requests types – presumably *get* requests – we'll simply display the search input page.

Once we know that we have a post request, what is the rest of this code doing? Well, it's another example of Grails's ability to provide significant functionality in a few succinct commands. For all *post* requests, the search action will...

- Get the search criteria from the request using `params.city`.
- Get a list of `Race` objects for races matching that city using the `findAllByCityLike` method – just one of the many available dynamic finder methods.
- Put the results in an object named `raceList`.
- `render` the view, using the `raceList` object as the `model`, in the `list` view template. (Because we just want to display a list of matching races, we can safely use the existing *Race List* template – `racetrack/grails-app/views/race/list.gsp`.)

When we click *Search*, sure enough, we get the matching results.

Of course, if we can search races by city, why not search by state as well? We can easily add a new input field to our search page for this purpose.

```
<tr class='prop'>
    <td valign='top' class='name'>
        <label for='state'>State:</label>
    </td>
    <td valign='top' class='value'>
        <g:select name='state'
from='${[""] + new Race().constraints.state.inList}'>
        </g:select>
    </td>
</tr>
```

A simple text input field was perfectly appropriate for entering the city, but a select field is better suited for capturing the state parameter. However, in order to build a select field, we have to know the valid options. We certainly don't want to hard code the list of states in the page, so luckily we can obtain the list of valid states right from our domain class – the definitive source for this information. And because the user may not always want to query by state, we add a blank value as the first option in the list.

That was easy enough, but what do we have to change in our controller? As it turns out, there's actually very little we need to change. Instead of using the findAllByCityNameLike method, we'll now invoke another dynamic finder –

findAllByCityLikeAndStateLike.

```
def search = {
  if (request.method == 'POST') {
    render( view:'list',
            model:[raceList:
                      Race.findAllByCityLikeAndStateLike
                          ('%' + params.city + '%',
                           '%' + params.state + '%')
                  ]
          )
  }
}
```

Grails automatically provides dynamic finders for just about every query combination you can think of! Try it out. Our search from above now yields just what we'd expect given our updated query.

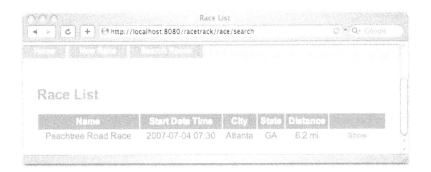

Build Your Own Criteria

Over time, we'll likely see our requirements grow in complexity. (That's good though. It keeps us on our toes.) So, how can we support additional query parameters with different data types and different conditional operators? For example, suppose I want to find all races where the distance is *at least* 5 miles and the date is *between* July 1st and September 15th. That kind of query is beyond the capabilities of the dynamic finders that we just saw. No worries, though. That doesn't mean that your application has to take on any additional complexity. Grails offers the immensely flexible Hibernate Criteria Builder[23] to satisfy that need without sacrificing any of the functionality we've seen so far.

Quick Note: If you don't anticipate needing to support these types of queries in your applications, you can safely skip ahead to Chapter 6 for now. Feel free to refer back to this section if your needs change.

Introducing the Hibernate Criteria Builder

Before we add any new query parameters, let's take a moment to first understand the structure of a Hibernate Criteria Builder. To do so, we'll migrate the existing `search` action to use a Hibernate Criteria Builder instead of the current dynamic finder.

```
def search = {
    if (request.method == 'POST') {
        def criteria = Race.createCriteria()

        def results = criteria {
            and {
                like('city', '%' + params.city + '%')
                like('state', '%' + params.state + '%')
            }
        }

        render(view:'list', model:[ raceList: results ])
    }
}
```

Even if you've never used Hibernate or Grails before, you can quickly get the gist of what's going on here. A Hibernate Criteria Builder is one kind of Groovy builder, and in a Groovy builder, each component is referred to as a "node." The `and` node tells us that we'll match any records that satisfy one or more of the criteria specified by its child nodes. In this case, it has two child nodes.

The first child node returns results that satisfy a case-insensitive
`like` operation on the `city` attribute.

```
like('city', '%' + params.city + '%')
```

Similarly, the second child node applies a case-insensitive `like`
operation on the `state` attribute.

```
like('state', '%' + params.state + '%')
```

Together, these nodes are equivalent to the dynamic finder we
used previously. However, now we can easily expand this
builder to support more advanced query requirements.

If the builder structure seems oddly organized at first, it's
because the Hibernate Criteria Builder somewhat resembles a
Polish notation syntax, in which you specify the operator *before*
the operands.[24] That's certainly a departure from Java's use of
relational operators, but it should become relatively intuitive
after your first few queries.

Enhancing the View

Now, let's modify our search page to capture the input for our
new requirements. If we edit `search.gsp` and add the following
input fields, it should give us what we're looking for.

```
<tr class='prop'>
    <td valign='top' class='name'>
        <label for='date'>Date:</label>
    </td>
    <td valign='top' class='value'>
        between
        <g:datePicker name='minDate' precision='day' />
        and
        <g:datePicker name='maxDate' precision='day'
            value='${new Date().plus(365*2)}'/>
    </td>
</tr>
<tr class='prop'>
    <td valign='top' class='name'>
        <label for='distance'>Distance:</label>
    </td>
    <td valign='top' class='value'>
        <select name='distanceOperator' >
            <option value='AT_LEAST' >At least</option>
```

```
                    <option value='EXACTLY' >Exactly</option>
                    <option value='AT_MOST' >At most</option>
                </select>
                <input type='text' name='distance' size='5'>
                </input> mi
            </td>
        </tr>
```

And a quick sanity check tells us that we're on the right track.

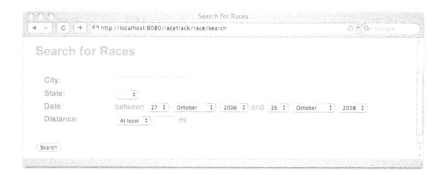

Working with Java Classes

You'll notice that we're now capturing query parameters that do not map directly to our domain class. For example, our query parameters now include a minimum date and a maximum date, but our domain class simply contains a single date – *the* starting date/time for the race. Similarly, we now have a new query operator (i.e., *at least*, *exactly*, or *at most*) associated with the race distance, but the actual race domain model only has the race distance. In short, we lack a nice one-to-one mapping between the domain model and the data parameters that make up the query request. In these situations, I prefer to define a class to represent the query itself. Let's add a `RaceQuery` class to fulfill this need.

Where does such a class belong in our project structure? It's not a domain class per se, because we have no need to persist one of these query objects. It's not a controller, and it's certainly not a view. This is where the `racetrack/src` directory comes into play. It's in this directory that we can add Groovy or Java classes for use by our Grails application.

The distance operator has exactly three valid values – *at least*, *exactly*, or *at most* – thus making it a perfect candidate for an enumerated type. And if we want to use enumerated types, we'll need to implement the RaceQuery class in Java. (Groovy will eventually support enumerated types, but we'll have to wait for Groovy 2.0.[25])

Java 5 Dependency Note: If you're using a JDK prior to Java 5, you'll need to use an alternate mechanism (e.g., a java.lang.String object) for capturing the distance operator value.

Without further ado, let's implement this new class – RaceQuery.java – and place it in the racetrack/src/java directory.

```java
import java.util.Date;

public class RaceQuery {
    public enum DistanceOperator {AT_LEAST,EXACTLY,AT_MOST};

    private Date minDate;
    private Date maxDate;
    private String city;
    private String state;
    private Float distance;
    private DistanceOperator distanceOperator;

    public String getCity() {
        return city;
    }

    public void setCity(String city) {
        this.city = city;
    }
    // remaining getters and setters not shown
    // ...
}
```

Now that we have a class for capturing the query parameters, we're ready to put it to use in the builder.

Expanding the Criteria Builder

Let's update the builder to work with our new query object and the new query parameters that it provides. (This code should replace our current `search` action in `RaceController.groovy`.)

```groovy
def search = {
   if (request.method == 'POST') {
      RaceQuery query = new RaceQuery()
      bindData(query, params)

      def criteria = Race.createCriteria()

      def results = criteria {
         and {
            like('city', '%' + query.city + '%')
            like('state', '%' + query.state + '%')
            if (query.distance) {
               switch (query.distanceOperator) {
                  case RaceQuery.DistanceOperator.AT_LEAST:
                     ge('distance', query.distance)
                     break
                  case RaceQuery.DistanceOperator.EXACTLY:
                     eq('distance', query.distance)
                     break
                  case RaceQuery.DistanceOperator.AT_MOST:
                     le('distance', query.distance)
                     break
                  default:
                     log.error "Found unexpected value for
                                distance"
                        + " operator -
                          ${query.distanceOperator}"
               }
            }

            // Add 1 day (24 hours) to the max date.
            // (If user selects a max date of Jan 1st,
            // the date object will hold Jan 1st 00:00,
            // but the user will want any events
            // occurring thru Jan 1st 23:59.)
            between('startDateTime',
                    query.minDate,
                    query.maxDate + 1)
         } //and
      }
      render(view:'list', model:[ raceList: results ])
   } //if
}
```

Now that we've seen the code, let's walk through the individual changes we made to get this action to work with the `RaceQuery` object and the new parameters.

- First, we added code to instantiate a new `RaceQuery` object and bind the request parameters to the `RaceQuery` object. Grails provides the dynamic `bindData` method to all controllers. This method interrogates the request parameters and the target object – in this case, a `RaceQuery` object – and populates the target object with the corresponding parameters (determined by name) in the request, conveniently performing type conversion as needed.

```
RaceQuery query = new RaceQuery()
bindData(query, params)
```

- Next, we added logic to include the distance-related parameters in the builder. The `switch` statement evaluates the `distanceOperator` attribute and adds the appropriate node to the builder. For example, if the query is looking for races that are *at least* 5 miles long, the builder will include a `ge` node to identify races with distances greater than or equal to the specified distance.

```
ge('distance', query.distance)
```

- Lastly, we included new code to incorporate the date-related parameters into the builder. The `between` node matches races with a start date occurring between the specified minimum and maximum dates (inclusively).

```
between('startDateTime', query.minDate, query.maxDate + 1)
```

Now let's see it in action. First, we need to restart the application to pick up the new `RaceQuery` class. Then, we're ready to try it out. Recall that we wanted to find all races where the distance is *at least* 5 miles and the date is *between* July 1st and September 15th.

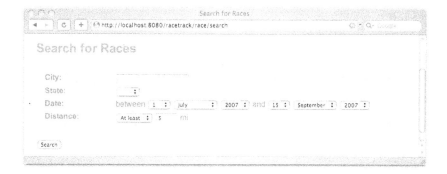

And when we click *Search*, we get exactly that.

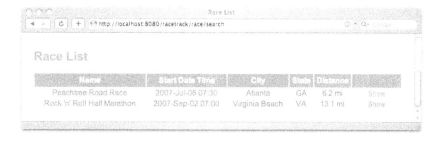

6

Not Just for Intranet Apps

So far, we've managed to put together a fully functioning application for managing races and registrations, but do we really want our *internal* team to have to manually enter all the registrations for every runner? Wouldn't we rather allow runners to register themselves? Certainly. But opening the application to external users brings with it some additional considerations.

- Public users versus administrators – Administrators (i.e., internal users) should continue to have access to all of the functionality we've built so far. We'd like to allow public users (i.e., non-administrators) to search for races and register themselves for races (assuming registration is not yet full for the race in question), but that's where their access should end. We need to protect the application's administrative features, and only allow the internal users to access that functionality.

- Authentication – In order to allow different levels of functionality for different users, we need a way to distinguish an administrator from a non-administrator. This, of course, calls for an authentication mechanism to allow administrators to submit their credentials.

- Look-and-feel – The Grails templates we've used so far were certainly good enough for our intranet app (and are still good enough for the administrative features), but we'll want to provide a more customized look-and-feel for the public portion of our application.

69

After sitting down with our customers to understand their needs, we've sketched out a basic flow for the public portion of the application.

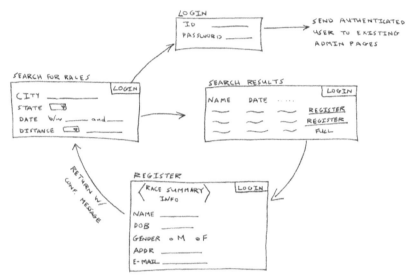

Figure 6-1: User Interface Flow for Public-Facing Pages

Beyond CRUD

Changing the Landing Page

Whenever a user accesses the root URL (http://localhost:8080/racetrack), we want the application to display the *Search for Races* page as the new default landing page. (We don't want our public users to see the current landing page that simply prompts the user to select a controller.) All requests to the root URL are handled by `racetrack/web-app/index.jsp`. When you open this file in your editor, you'll see the content used to generate the current landing page. Replace the existing content with the following line.

```
<%response.sendRedirect(request.getContextPath()+"/race/search");
%>
```

As you can see, `index.jsp` will now redirect to the *Search for Races* page at http://localhost:8080/racetrack/race/search.

Adding Public-Friendly Views

Next, we need to add the pages that our public users will access to view the races matching their search criteria and to register for a race. We can't simply use the existing pages that offer this functionality, because those pages also include various administrative features. For example, the current page that displays the list of races also allows the user to create a new race, but we only want administrators to have that sort of access. Our public users need a read-only view of races with no options to create, update, or delete any records.

We could conceivably make the existing *Race List* page smart enough to distinguish an administrator from a non-administrator, but doing so assumes that we'll always want the administrator's view to look fairly similar to the public view. That's probably not a safe assumption, so let's add a new template –
`racetrack/grails-app/views/race/ searchresults.gsp` – to provide the public view of this data.

```
<html>
<head>
<meta http-equiv="Content-Type"content="text/html;
        charset=UTF-8"/>
<meta name="layout" content="main" />
    <title>Races Meeting Your Criteria</title>
</head>
<body>
    <div class="body">
        <h1>Search Results</h1>
        <h2>
        <g:if test="${raceList?.size() == 1}">
            1 Race Meets Your Criteria:
        </g:if>
        <g:else>
            ${raceList?.size()} Races Meet Your Criteria:
        </g:else>
        </h2>
        <g:if test="${flash.message}">
            <div class="message">${flash.message}</div>
        </g:if>
        <div class="dialog">
        <table>
            <tr>
                <th>Name</th>
                <th nowrap>Start Date</th>
                <th nowrap>Start Time</th>
                <th>City</th>
```

```
            <th>State</th>
            <th>Distance</th>
            <th>Cost</th>
            <th></th>
        </tr>
        <g:each in="${raceList}">
        <tr>
            <td nowrap>
                <span class="lineItemValue">${it.name}</span>
            </td>
            <td nowrap>
                <span class="lineItemValue">
                <g:formatDate date="${it.startDateTime}"
                    format="EEE, MMM d, yyyy"/>
                </span>
            </td>
            <td nowrap>
                <span class="lineItemValue">
                <g:formatDate date="${it.startDateTime}"
                            format="h:mm a z"/>
                </span>
            </td nowrap>
            <td nowrap>
                <span class="lineItemValue">${it.city}</span>
            </td>
            <td nowrap>
                <span class="lineItemValue">${it.state}</span>
            </td>
            <td nowrap class="numericData">
                <span class="lineItemValue">
                  <g:formatNumber number="${it.distance}"
                            format="##0.0 mi"/>
                </span>
            </td>
            <td nowrap class="numericData">
                <span class="lineItemValue">
                   <g:formatNumber number="${it.cost}"
                            format="\$0.00"/>
                </span>
            </td>
            <td class="actionButtons">
                <g:if test="${
                    it.registrations?.size() < it.maxRunners}">
                    <span class="actionButton">
                      <g:link controller="registration"
                            action="register"
                            id="${it.id}">Register
                      </g:link>
                    </span>
                </g:if>
                <g:else><strong>Full<strong></g:else>
            </td>
        </tr>
        </g:each>
    </table>
    </div>
  </div>
</body>
</html>
```

Now we need to modify `RaceController.groovy` to render the view using this new template instead of the existing `list.gsp` template. In the `search` action, simply change the name of the view from `list` to `searchresults`.

```
render(view:'searchresults', model:[ raceList: results ])
```

We've defined a new view and we've updated the controller, so we're ready to try out our changes.

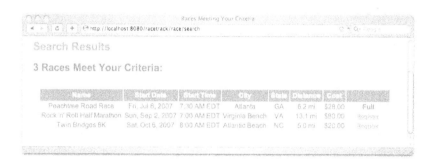

We now have a reasonable read-only view for our public users. And as an added touch, the right-most column also now includes an indication of whether the user can still register for a given race.

Speaking of registering for races, you may have noticed that we asked the *Register* link (in `searchresults.gsp`) to route its requests to the `register` action in `RegistrationController`.

```
<g:link controller="registration"
    action="register" id="${it.id}">Register
</g:link>
```

We don't have a `register` action yet, so let's define one in `RegistrationController.groovy`.

```
def register = {
    def registration = new Registration()
    registration.properties = params

    if (request.method == 'GET') {
        def race = Race.get(params.id)
        return ['registration':registration,'race':race]
```

```
        }
    else {
        if(registration.save()) {
            flash.message =
                "Successfully registered for
                 ${registration.race.name}"
            redirect(controller:'race',action:'search')
        }
        else {
            def race = Race.get(params['race.id'])
            return
                ['registration':registration,'race':race]
        }
    }
}
}
```

Following an approach similar to the one we used for the search
action in RaceController.groovy, the register action will
interrogate the request type to determine how to process the
request.

For *get* requests, the action will simply display the registration
page for the given race. The template will have access to the
Registration object and the Race object for use in rendering
the page.

For *post* requests, the action will attempt to persist the
Registration object (populated from the request parameters).
If it's able to validate and save the registration successfully, then
the action will route the user back to the search page and display
a friendly confirmation message. Otherwise, the action will
redisplay the registration input page and alert the user to the
problems that prevented the application from saving the
registration.

As we now know, upon exiting from the register action, by
convention Grails will look for the corresponding view template
at racetrack/grails-
app/views/registration/register.gsp. Since we're effect-
ively just creating a new registration, we can borrow much of the
structure for this new template from create.gsp. However,
because we want to make this page available to our non-

administrative users, we'll be sure to customize the template accordingly.

```
<html>
  <head>
    <meta http-equiv="Content-Type" content="text/html;
charset=UTF-8"/>
    <meta name="layout" content="main" />
    <title>Register</title>
  </head>
  <body>
  <div class="body">
      <h1>Register for ${race.name} </h1>
      <em>Start Date:
        <g:formatDate date="${race.startDateTime}"
                      format="EEE, MMM d, yyyy"/>
        <br />
      </em>
      <em>Start Time:
        <g:formatDate date="${race.startDateTime}"
          format="h:mm a z"/>
        <br />
      </em>
      <g:if test="${flash.message}">
        <div class="message">${flash.message}</div>
      </g:if>
      <g:hasErrors bean="${registration}">
        <div class="errors">
          <g:renderErrors bean="${registration}" as="list" />
        </div>
      </g:hasErrors>
      <g:form action="register" method="post" >
        <g:hiddenField name="race.id" value="${race.id}" />
        <div class="dialog">
        <table>
          <tr class='prop'>
            <td valign='top' class='name'>
              <label for='name'>Name:</label>
          </td>
            <td valign='top'
            class='value
${hasErrors(bean:registration,field:'name','errors')}'>
              <input type="text" maxlength='50' name='name'
                value='${registration?.name}'></input>
          </td>
        </tr>
          <tr class='prop'>
            <td valign='top' class='name'>
              <label for='dateOfBirth'>Date Of Birth:</label>
          </td>
            <td valign='top'
            class='value
${hasErrors(bean:registration,field:'dateOfBirth','errors')}'>
              <g:datePicker name='dateOfBirth'
                            value='${registration?.dateOfBirth}'
                            precision='day'></g:datePicker>
          </td>
```

```
        </tr>
        <tr class='prop'>
          <td valign='top' class='name'>
            <label for='gender'>Gender:</label>
          </td>
          <td valign='top' class='value
${hasErrors(bean:registration,field:'gender','errors')}'>
              <g:radio name='gender' value='M'
                checked='${registration?.gender?.equals("M")}' >
               </g:radio>
               Male
              <g:radio name='gender' value='F'
                checked='${registration?.gender?.equals("F")}' >
               </g:radio>
               Female
          </td>
        </tr>
        <tr class='prop'>
          <td valign='top' class='name'>
            <label for='postalAddress'>Postal Address:</label>
          </td>
          <td valign='top'
          class='value
${hasErrors(bean:registration,field:'postalAddress','errors')}'>
              <textarea rows='3' cols='30' name='postalAddress'>
                ${registration?.postalAddress}
              </textarea>
          </td>
        </tr>
        <tr class='prop'>
          <td valign='top' class='name'>
            <label for='emailAddress'>Email Address:</label>
          </td>
          <td valign='top'
          class='value
${hasErrors(bean:registration,field:'emailAddress','errors')}'>
              <input type="text" maxlength='50'
name='emailAddress'
                value='${registration?.emailAddress}'></input>
          </td>
        </tr>
      </table>
    </div>
    <div class="buttons">
      <input type="submit" value="Register"
            class="formbutton"></input>
      <input type="button" value="Cancel"
            onClick="history.back()"
            class="formbutton">
      </input>
    </div>
  </g:form>
</div>
</body>
</html>
```

Now when a user registers for a race, the registration page will include the race name, date, and time, but it will hide the other administrative CRUD functions that only internal users can perform.

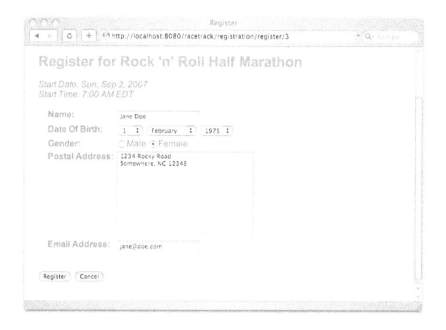

And assuming the user enters valid information, she'll be greeted with message confirming her registration. She can go lace up and start training!

Implementing User Authentication

We now have all the pages we want to make available to our public users, but it's certainly not enough to just trust that they'll stay away from the administrative components. No, we need to put some security in place to restrict access to those non-public features. To do so, we'll first need a way for our administrative users to authenticate themselves to the application. Once authenticated, they'll be able to access the secured areas of the system.

Managing User Accounts

Knowing that we'll need to maintain a list of authorized users and their credentials, why not just define a new Grails domain class to support that data? Using the approach we demonstrated earlier for the `Race` and `Registration` classes, let's create a `User` domain class with the following attributes and constraints.

```
class User {
    String userId
    String password

    static constraints = {
        userId(length:6..8,unique:true)
        password(length:6..8)
    }
}
```

Quick Note: For a secure production application, we wouldn't dare use plain text passwords. Instead, we'd likely opt for a one-way encryption algorithm (such as SHA[26]) to allow us to work with hashed passwords. We won't go into those details here, but you can have a look at Java's `MessageDigest`[27] class for more information on using secure one-way hash functions in Java (and/or Grails) applications.

Now that we have the domain class in place, use the `grails generate-all` command to generate the user interface scaffolding to manage the user data.

Before we lock down the administrative features, we first need to create at least one administrator for the application. While we could just use the user interface to create the first administrator, there's another option that offers some additional benefits.

Grails provides a bootstrap mechanism for performing any initialization tasks that you want your application to perform at startup.[28] By convention, Grails looks for classes in the `racetrack/grails-app/conf` directory with names like `FooBootStrap.groovy`, `BarBootStrap.groovy`, etc. Grails expects these classes to contain an `init` closure – to be called on application startup – and a `destroy` closure – to be invoked as the application shuts down. (As a general rule, you don't want to rely on the `destroy` closure to perform any mission-critical work. If for some reason the application terminates abnormally, the `destroy` closure is not guaranteed to run.)

By default, Grails provides an empty bootstrap class for us to use as we see fit. Let's use that class – `racetrack/grails-app/conf/ApplicationBootStrap.groovy` – to create the first administrator.

```
class ApplicationBootStrap {
    def init = { servletContext ->
        final String BACKUP_ADMIN = 'adminjoe'
        if (!User.findByUserId(BACKUP_ADMIN)) {

new User(userId:BACKUP_ADMIN,password:'password').save()

        }
    }

    def destroy = {
    }
}
```

Because this closure runs each time the application starts, we can rest assured that we'll always have at least one administrator defined at application startup. We'll never be left unable to log in. (Of course, we don't want duplicate user entries, so our code first makes sure the user does not already exist before creating it.)

Intercepting and Authenticating

If we expect our administrators to log in to the system, we obviously need to give them a place to do so. Let's add a new template — `racetrack/grails-app/views/user/` `login.gsp` — to serve as the authentication page.

```
<html>
<head>
<meta http-equiv="Content-Type" content="text/html;
      charset=UTF-8"/>
<meta name="layout" content="main" />
<title>Log in</title>
</head>
    <body>
        <div class="body">
            <h1>Please log in</h1>
            <g:if test="${flash.message}">
                <div class="message">${flash.message}</div>
            </g:if>
            <g:hasErrors bean="${race}">
                <div class="errors">
                    <g:renderErrors bean="${user}" as="list" />
                </div>
            </g:hasErrors>
            <g:form controller="user" method="post" >
                <div class="dialog">
                <table>
                    <tr class='prop'>
                        <td valign='top' class='name'>
                            <label for='userId'>User ID:</label>
                        </td>
                        <td valign='top' class='value '>
                            <input type="text" maxlength='8'
                                    name='userId'
                                    value='${user?.userId}'>
                            </input>
                        </td>
                    </tr>
                    <tr class='prop'>
                        <td valign='top' class='name'>
                          <label for='password'>Password:</label>
                        </td>
                        <td valign='top' class='value '>
                            <input type="password" maxlength='8'
                                    name='password'
                                    value='${user?.password}'>
                            </input>
                        </td>
                    </tr>
                </table>
                </div>

                <div class="buttons">
                <span class="button">
                  <g:actionSubmit value="Log in" />
```

```
                    </span>
                    </div>
                </g:form>
            </div>
        </body>
</html>
```

And next, we need actions to render the login page and to process the requests coming from the login page. As we've seen before, we can handle different request types from a single action, so we'll continue that pattern here as well. Let's add the following action to the UserController class.

```
def login = {
    if (request.method == "GET") {
        session.userId = null
        def user = new User()
    }
    else {
        def user =
User.findByUserIdAndPassword(params.userId,
                              params.password)
        if (user) {
            session.userId = user.userId
            redirect(controller:'race')
        }
        else {
flash['message'] = 'Please enter a valid user ID and password'
        }
    }
}
```

Our application will use a simple (yet effective) approach for identifying a logged-in user. When a user successfully logs in, we store the user ID in the session (in a parameter named "userId"). When the user logs out – as we'll see in a moment – we remove the user ID from the session. At any given time, the application can look for the user ID in the session to determine whether the user is logged-in.

When the login action receives a *get* request, this indicates that the user is trying to log in. In case the user is already logged-in for some reason – perhaps the user is trying to log in under a different account – we'll first make sure that session.userId is null and then render the login page.

When the user submits her user ID and password, the `login` action will receive a *post* request, and we need to validate the user's entries. We look for a user with that ID and password, and if such a user exists, we add the user ID to the session and send the user to the *Race List* page. If we don't find a user with that ID and password, then we return the user to the login page and kindly ask them to stop trying to hack into our application.

Before we leave the `UserController` class, we need to give our users a way to log out of the application. Let's add a `logout` action to remove the user ID from the session and then return the user to the public portion of the application with a friendly confirmation message.

```
def logout = {
    session.userId = null
    flash['message'] = 'Successfully logged out'
    redirect(controller:'race', action:'search')
}
```

Adding Interceptors

Now we need a way to intercept access to any administrative areas of the application and force the user to first log in before proceeding to those areas. In short, we want to restrict access to all functionality except the few public-friendly modules we implemented a short while ago. Grails action interceptors provide a convenient mechanism for implementing this feature.[29]

Action interceptors – plainly enough – intercept the normal flow of execution for an action and allow us to perform some other functionality before or after the action executes. For security purposes, before a user can perform some administrative activity, we first want to make sure the user is an administrator. Therefore, we need a `beforeInterceptor` to invoke our authentication module before executing any administrative actions.

Let's assume that we'll define a method named `auth` to determine whether a user has logged in to the application. In the `RaceController` class, we want that method to execute before every action except the search action (because we want to allow public access to the search action). We achieve this functionality with the simple declaration below.

```
class RaceController {
    def beforeInterceptor = [action:this.&auth,
                             except:['search']]

    //...
}
```

This declaration tells Grails, "For every action except search, invoke the auth method before passing control to the action." Of course, we still need an auth method, but we'll come to that shortly. First, let's add the necessary interceptors to the other two controllers.

In RegistrationController.groovy, public users can only access the register action. Users must authenticate before accessing any other actions.

```
class RegistrationController {
    def beforeInterceptor = [action:this.&auth,
                             except:'register']

    //...
}
```

In the UserController class, we want to restrict access to everything except the login and logout actions.

```
class UserController {
    def beforeInterceptor = [action:this.&auth,
                             except:['login', 'logout']]

    //...
}
```

We should also note that while the above interceptors apply to all of the controllers' actions *except* the named actions, Grails also allows us to define an interceptor that will execute *only* for a list of named actions. For example...

```
def beforeInterceptor = [action:this.&auth,
                         only:['fooaction', 'baraction']]
```

Introducing a BaseController

All of our controllers now rely on a yet-to-be-defined `auth`
method, but we obviously don't want to duplicate this method in
every controller. It's therefore time to introduce an abstract
parent class for our controllers and define the `auth` method
there. We'll name this class `BaseController` and define it in
`racetrack/grails-app/controllers/`
`BaseController.groovy`.

```
abstract class BaseController {
    def auth() {
        if(!session.userId) {
            redirect(controller:'user',action:'login')
            return false
        }
    }
}
```

Application-wide, we know that we can identify a logged-in user
by looking for the user ID in the session. The `auth` method
relies on this rule to determine where to route a request.

If the user ID is not present in the session, then we know the user
is not logged-in. We redirect the user to the login page and
return `false`. Recall that this method is called from an
interceptor before passing control to the requested action. By
returning `false`, we inform Grails that we are overriding the
normal flow of execution and that it should not to proceed to the
originally-requested action.

If, on the other hand, the user ID is present in the session, then
we know that the user is logged-in, and we simply exit from the
`auth` method. Grails then proceeds on to the intercepted action.

Now that we have the `BaseController` class, we need to update
our existing controllers to inherit its functionality.

```
class RaceController extends BaseController {
//...
}

class RegistrationController extends BaseController {
//...
}

class UserController extends BaseController {
//...
}
```

Whew! That was a tad more than we'd probably prefer to do without some intermediate testing, so let's not wait any longer. Let's start up the application and try to sneak into one of the newly-restricted areas of the system. We know that only administrators can create races, so we'll see if our security will keep Joe Public away from that module. When we try to access http://localhost:8080/racetrack/race/create, what will we see?

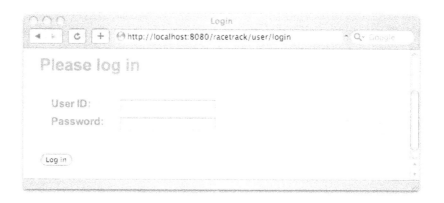

Good. When an unauthenticated user tries to access an administrative portion of the site, the application now asks the user to first log in. That's just what we wanted.

Before we move on, spend a few minutes experimenting with our new security system. Make sure we can still access the public areas of the application without logging in. Verify that we can log out successfully. Make sure you can't get in with a bogus password.

Done? OK. So, yes, the security module does its job, but doesn't the user experience feel a bit awkward now? Did you notice that the application always takes you to the *Race List* page after logging in – regardless of which page you were trying to access? What about navigation in general? There's no user-friendly way to get from the public area of the app to the race administration area, to the user administration area, etc. We can do better than that.

Improving Our Memory

When we see a user trying to access a restricted area of the application and the user isn't logged-in yet, we route the user to the login page, and we do a terrible thing along the way. We completely forget where the user was trying to go. Instead, we should take a snapshot of the user's request so that once the user logs in, we can continue with the original request.

Inside the `auth` method (in `BaseController.groovy`), add the new code shown below to save the request until we're ready to process it. We first build a map with the controller name and action name, and we then fill the map with all of the parameters from the request. Just before we send the user to the login page, we store the map in the session for safekeeping.

```
def auth() {
    if(!session.userId) {
        def originalRequestParams =
            [controller:controllerName,
            action:actionName]

        originalRequestParams.putAll(params)

        session.originalRequestParams =
            originalRequestParams

        redirect(controller:'user',action:'login')
        return false
    }
}
```

On the other end of this equation lies the `login` action in the `UserController` class. Once the user logs in, we simply fetch the details of the original request and proceed to process it. (As a safeguard, we send the user to the *Race List* page if for some reason we can't find the original request.)

```
def login = {
    if (request.method == 'GET') {
        //...
    }
    else {
        def user =

User.findByUserIdAndPassword(params.userId,
                                 params.password)
        if (user) {
            session.userId = user.userId

            def redirectParams =
                session.originalRequestParams ?
                session.originalRequestParams :
                [controller:'race']
            redirect(redirectParams)
        }
        //...
    }
}
```

Take a moment to restart the application to pick up these changes. Now when someone tries to access a protected resource (e.g., http://localhost:8080/racetrack/race/create), we're kind enough to take the user to that resource once she logs in.

May I See a Menu, Please?

The functionality we provide to our public users is simple enough that they can get by without a menu. They simply search for races, select from a list, and then register. Our administrators, however, have several additional options. Assuming we want to make the menu available on all pages, how can we avoid adding the individual menu options to each and every template? Grails allows us to define sub-templates – used to render just a portion of a page – that we can then embed in other view templates. Because we can reuse a sub-template wherever we like, one should work well for providing our new menu.

We distinguish a sub-template from standard templates by – you guessed it – convention. Let's assume we'd like to refer to our menu sub-template as `adminmenubar`. Then, by convention, we need to define this template in a file named `_adminmenubar.gsp`. To determine where this file should reside, we first need to consider which templates will include this sub-template. If we only wanted to access the sub-template in the race-related views, we would place the sub-template in `racetrack/grails-app/views/race`. However, because we want to access it from all views, we need to place the sub-template in the root view directory – `racetrack/grails-app/views`.

Inside the sub-template, we'll determine whether the user is logged-in and display the menu options accordingly.

```
<g:if test="${!session.userId}">
    <span class="menuButton">
        <g:link controller="user" action="login">Log
in</g:link>
    </span>
</g:if>
<g:else>
    <span class="menuButton">
        <g:link controller="race" action="list">
            Manage Races & Registrations
        </g:link>
    </span>
    <span class="menuButton">
        <g:link controller="user" action="list">
            Manage Administrators
        </g:link>
    </span>
    <span class="menuButton">
        <g:link controller="user" action="logout">
            Log out
        </g:link>
    </span>
</g:else>
```

Now, in order to add the menu to the appropriate pages, we simply refer to the sub-template. Let's start with the page that serves as the entry point into the application – the *Search for Races* page. Add the content shown below to `racetrack/grails-app/ views/race/search.gsp`. The `<g:render>` tag will evaluate the contents of the sub-template and include the results at this location in the page.

```
<html>
    ...
    <body>
        <div class="nav">
            <g:render template="/adminmenubar" />
        </div>
        ...
    </body>
</html>
```

Notice that we did not include the leading underscore when referring to the sub-template in the `<g:render>` tag. This tag is used exclusively for rendering sub-templates, so it will automatically prepend the underscore when looking for the GSP.

Also notice that we include a forward slash before the template name. The forward slash tells Grails to look for the template in the root view directory. Without the slash, Grails would expect to find the sub-template in the same directory as the referring template.

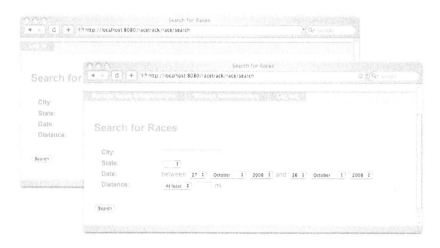

We can now add the menu to the application's other pages as well. By defining the menu just once and including a reference to it (using the `<g:render>` tag) in other pages, we can manage changes to the menu from a single location. When we modify the sub-template, all pages that include the sub-template will automatically reflect the change.

Are you asking yourself why the heck we had to update all the pages to refer to the sub-template? Good. You're right to ask that question. Even though we're not including the details of the menu-generation code in every template, this is still a less-than-ideal solution. In fact, if we were building the application from scratch (or we wanted to perform more significant surgery on the scaffolding-generated views), we could have just placed the menu in the main layout –

`racetrack/grails-app/views/layouts/main.gsp`. The main layout currently provides other common components we see on each page (e.g., the logo, the stylesheet, etc.), so we could have easily included the menu in the main layout as well. We'll look at this approach more closely in the next section.

UI Makeover: Layouts and CSS

When the conversation turns to how an application *looks*, that's usually a good sign. It typically means that we've done well as developers and the site *functions* well enough for the customer to start to focus on aesthetics. So, let's step up a notch from the default Grails look-and-feel and give our end-users a more customized interface.

Our makeover will consist of three main steps. For starters, we'll define a customized style sheet with the look-and-feel we want for the public portion of the site. Then, we'll add a few images to the project to support the new look. Lastly, we'll define a separate layout template for the public pages to use. Ready? Let's go.

First, let's add the new stylesheet to the application. Grails looks for stylesheets in `racetrack/web-app/css/`, so we need to place the new stylesheet – `public.css` – in that directory. (For the sake of brevity, the stylesheet contents are not included the text of this book However, the full stylesheet – along with the complete source code for all examples in this book – is available for you to download and follow along.[3])

Our new stylesheet references four new images – `banner.jpg`, `bg.gif`, `formbg.gif`, and `transrace.png`. So, next we need to copy those images into the `racetrack/web-app/images` directory.

```
racetrack> ls -1 web-app/images/
banner.jpg
bg.gif
formbg.gif
grails_logo.jpg
spinner.gif
transrace.png
tree
```

Now that we have those items taken care of, let's take a moment to discuss layouts. Did you notice that none of the templates we've worked with in this application made any mention of a stylesheet? Did you notice that none of those templates referenced the Grails logo that we see on every page? If the templates don't include that information, then why do we clearly see the logo and the effects of a stylesheet when the pages are rendered in the browser? The answer lies in a single tag included in each of the templates.

```
...
<head>
    <meta http-equiv="Content-Type" content="text/html;
        charset=UTF-8"/>
    <meta name="layout" content="main" />
    <title>Some Title</title>
</head>
...
```

This tag tells Grails to render the template using the layout named `main`. Grails then expects to find the layout template – `main.gsp` – in the application's global layout directory – `racetrack/grails-app/views/layouts`. We use a layout to define the general structure we want to apply to a site (or a subset of the pages in a site), and we refer to that layout from the templates that wish to use it (either explicitly using the `meta` tag or by convention[30]). The template then concerns itself only with its specific content (e.g., a list of races), knowing that the layout will provide the framing around the page (e.g., the logo, common menus and links, etc.) as well as other items commonly needed by multiple templates (e.g., the stylesheet, common JavaScript functions, etc.).

Not only do layouts keep our application DRY, they also provide a one-stop shop for significantly rearranging the structure of our pages. For example, suppose we've defined the application's common menus as a series of horizontal tabs across the top of the page. Now, assume we later decide that the menu should instead appear as a vertical list along the left side of the page. If the layout contains the menu-rendering logic (as opposed to having the menu-rendering logic embedded separately in each template), we can change the layout and quickly see that change reflected across all pages that use the layout.

All of our application's pages currently use the default Grails layout template. Let's define a new custom layout for the public portion of the site. Create a new layout template at `racetrack/grails-app/views/layouts/public.gsp` and give it the following content.

```
<html>
    <head>
        <title><g:layoutTitle default="Racetrack" />
        </title>
        <link rel="stylesheet"
href="${createLinkTo(dir:'css',file:'public.css')}">
        </link>
        <g:layoutHead />
    </head>
    <body>
        <table class="contentArea">
            <tr>
                <td>
                    <div class="logo"></div>
                    <g:layoutBody />
                </td>
            </tr>
        </table>
    </body>
</html>
```

We can see that this layout references our new stylesheet. Also, look closely at the `<g:layoutTitle>`, `<g:layoutHead>`, and `<g:layoutBody>` tags. These tags serve as placeholders for the actual page content. At runtime, these tags pull in the corresponding content from the template that's using the layout. For example, when we change `search.gsp` to use this layout, at runtime Grails will render the content of the `<body>` tag in `seach.gsp` in place of the `<g:layoutBody>` tag in the layout template. (By the way, it's no coincidence that these tags bear a resemblance to the decorator tags in SiteMesh. In fact, Grails delegates this work to SiteMesh behind the scenes.)

Now that we have our new layout, the last step is to update the public pages to reference it instead of the default layout. In `search.gsp`, `searchresults.gsp`, and `register.gsp`, locate the tag that defines the layout, and change it to reference `public.gsp`.

```
<meta name="layout" content="public" />
```

And with that done, we're ready to reveal the new face of our application.

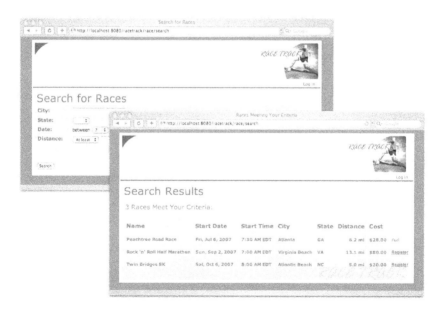

And there we have it, Folks. We've developed an application that our customers are happy with, and they're ready for us to push it into production! (Before we move on, you may have noticed that we have an opportunity to make our application a bit more DRY here. For extra credit, if we were to remove the `adminmenbar` reference from the three public page templates and place it instead in the layout template, then we could reduce some duplication in these pages. Are you up to the job?)

Putting It to the Test

There's no time for testing in *rapid* application development, right? Wrong! Remember the last time you used an application just because it was developed quickly? Of course not. We gravitate towards applications that work *well* and make us more productive, and we wish tax audits and root canals on those pitiful souls that try to force their buggy software on us. So, shame on us for waiting this long to talk about testing. (OK. I'll take the blame this time. You were just an innocent bystander.)

Unit Testing

Grails conveniently offers built-in support for unit testing. In fact, it might even make us feel a bit guilty for *not* testing. If we have a look in `racetrack/grails-tests`, we see that Grails has already created test classes for each of our domain models. The guilt is sure to set in when we look inside one of these classes, and we're quickly reminded that we have a whopping 0% test coverage so far.

```
class RaceTests extends GroovyTestCase {

    void testSomething() {

    }
}
```

It's time to fix that. (If you're new to writing unit tests in Groovy[31], you're in for a treat. Be careful. Once you try it, you may never want to go back.) First, let's decide what we need to test. The `RaceTests` class is where we'll include all the unit tests for the `Race` domain class. (We'll discuss the appropriate place for testing the controllers momentarily.) The Race class is fairly straightforward, but it does include more than just simple properties. Recall that we added several constraints to the class, and we even defined a custom constraint.

```
static constraints = {
    name(maxLength:50,blank:false)
    startDateTime(validator: {return (it > new Date())})
    city(maxLength:30,blank:false)
    state(inList:["GA", "NC", "SC", "VA"],blank:false)
    distance(min:3.1f,max:100f)
    cost(min:0f,max:999.99f)
}
```

I find it's useful to include test cases for the constraints. Even if you think you can look at the definition of the constraint and see that it's configured correctly, it's often valuable to actually write a few test cases to verify that those pesky edge cases are accounted for. Consider, for example, the custom constraint above for the startDateTime property. What happens if the date is null for some reason? (Is null greater than new Date()?) Well, we don't want any of our races to have a null starting date/time, so we should verify that the constraint will catch null values for us.

```
void testSomething() {
  def race = new Race()
  race.startDateTime = null

  assertFalse(race.validate())

  def fieldError = race.errors.getFieldError('startDateTime')
  def validationError = fieldError.codes.find {
          it == 'race.startDateTime.validator.invalid' }
  assertNotNull(validationError)
}
```

This test case creates a Race object with a null startDateTime property, asserts that the object validation fails, and then verifies that the errors include the expected error code for an invalid startDateTime property. Then, to run all test cases for our application, we simply enter grails test-app at the command prompt, and watch for the results.

```
racetrack> grails test-app
...
      [echo] Running tests for environment: test
...
      [java] OK (3 tests)
...
BUILD SUCCESSFUL
Total time: 11 seconds
```

Whew! We can rest a bit easier now knowing that we're adequately protected against null values in `startDateTime` property, but what about the other possible scenarios for our custom validator? Let's boost our confidence a bit more by including those test cases as well. (If you're wondering why Grails reported that 3 tests completed successfully, note that we have still have two embarrassingly bare test classes for our other domain classes. Those test cases – not surprisingly – passed as well.)

Let's add a test to make sure we also get a validation error when we specify a `startDateTime` property with a date/time value in the past. And, just as important as making sure we get errors for valid data, we also want to make sure we *don't* get any errors for a fully-valid `Race` object. If you want to get some extra assurance about the other constraints, you can include test cases for them as well. And, with a little bit of refactoring from our first test case, we can now quickly add new test cases for all sorts of scenarios.

```
class RaceTests extends GroovyTestCase {

  void testStartDateTimeCustomConstraintWithNullValue() {
      def race = getValidRace()
      race.startDateTime = null
      assertValidationError(race, 'startDateTime',
          'race.startDateTime.validator.invalid')
  }

  void testStartDateTimeCustomConstraintWithPastValue(){
      def race = getValidRace()
      race.startDateTime = new Date(0)
      assertValidationError(race, 'startDateTime',
          'race.startDateTime.validator.invalid')
  }

  void testNameMaxConstraint() {
      def race = getValidRace()
```

```
        race.name = 'It may very well take longer to' +
                    ' typeout the name of this race' +
                    ' than to just go run it.'
        assertValidationError(race, 'name',
                              'race.name.maxLength.exceeded')
    }

    //...

    private Race getValidRace() {
        def race = new Race()
        race.name = 'Fast 5K'

        // 1 day in the future
        race.startDateTime = new Date().plus(1)
        race.city = 'Somewhere'
        race.state = 'NC'
        race.distance = 3.1
        race.cost = 20.00
        race.maxRunners = 1000

        // Make sure that we have indeed constructed a
        // valid Race object
        assertTrue(race.validate())

        return race
    }

    private assertValidationError(race, fieldName,
                                  errorName) {
        assertFalse(race.validate())
        def fieldError =
            race.errors.getFieldError(fieldName)
        def validationError = fieldError.codes.find {
                             it == errorName }
        assertNotNull(validationError)
    }
}
```

And once we're happy with the test coverage, it's time to see whether our constraints are as bulletproof as we hope they are.

```
racetrack> grails test-app
...
    [echo] Running tests for environment: test
...
    [java] OK (19 tests)
...
BUILD SUCCESSFUL
Total time: 12 seconds
```

Of course, you can add test cases for functionality other than just constraints. If you have any tricky relationships or other persistence-related features, you may want to include test cases to cover those areas as well.

Before testing any database-related functionality, you'll first want to configure your test data source to point to your test database. Grails will allow you to run the tests using any data source you prefer[32]; however, you typically want a dedicated database where your tests have free reign over all data, without impacting development or (of course) production. In this case, we'd update `racetrack/grails-app/conf/TestDataSource.groovy` as follows. (Note that you'd need to change the `username` and `password` to the appropriate values for your MySQL account.)

```
class TestDataSource {
    boolean pooling = true
    String dbCreate = "update"
    String url = "jdbc:mysql://localhost/racetrack_test"
    String driverClassName = "com.mysql.jdbc.Driver"
    String username = "jason"
    String password = ""
}
```

As you may have noticed from the output of the `grails test-app` command, Grails uses the test data source by default. If you'd like to run the tests against an alternate data source, simply include the environment name (i.e. `dev`, `test`, or `prod`) in the command.

```
racetrack> grails dev test-app
...
     [echo] Running tests for environment: development
...
     [java] OK (19 tests)
...
BUILD SUCCESSFUL
Total time: 10 seconds
```

Functional Testing

For those seeking even more confidence in their application's robustness, Grails also includes support for functional testing. Canoo WebTest provides the framework for the functional tests, and you can use your test cases to validate the application behavior as the end users will see it. The test cases can navigate to various URLs, click on buttons, follow links, verify page content, etc. If you're interested in adding functional tests to your application (or just seeing how they work), the online documentation includes a tutorial that walks you through generating a functional test, customizing the test to your needs, running the tests, and viewing the resulting test reports.[33]

8

The Finish Line

We've completed this round of development. The application is working and our customers like what they see; however, they're not going to run the application off of our development system, so we still have some work to do. Let's get the application into production, and call it a day.

Logging

Once the application is in production, we'll likely want a way to monitor various aspects of the application's activity. We may want to gather statistics about how people are using the system, capture certain data for help in potential debugging scenarios, etc. Grails has built-in logging – using log4j – to help meet these needs.

Each Grails controller includes a dynamic `log` method that provides access to the standard log4j functionality.[34] Each application also includes a `log4j.properties` file for use in customizing the log output.

It's always a good idea to keep track of any unauthorized users trying to gain access to an application, so let's add some logging to monitor that activity. In the `UserController` class, the `login` action validates the given user ID and password against the table of authorized users. If we detect an invalid user ID and password combination, we want to log a warning and include the details of the attempted breach.

```
def login = {
    if (request.method == "GET") {
```

```
                 session.userId = null
                 def user = new User()
            }
        else {
            def user =
    User.findByUserIdAndPassword(params.userId,
                             params.password)
        if (user) {
            session.userId = user.userId
            def redirectParams =
                session.originalRequestParams ?
                session.originalRequestParams :
                    [controller:'race']
            redirect(redirectParams)
        }
        else {
            log.warn "Shields up! Somebody's trying " +
                "to hack through our rock-solid " +
                "DEFCON 1 security -- " +
                "User ID - $params.userId, " +
                "Password - $params.password"

            flash['message'] = 'Please enter a valid user'+
                             'ID and password'
        }
    }
  }
}
```

By default, Grails only logs errors, and all logging output goes to the console. Of course, in production we'd rather have this information written to a file or perhaps even e-mailed to the administrator. Log4j offers appenders for all sorts of logging destinations[35], but for our purposes, we'll record this output to a file.

Much like the separate data sources used for each environment, Grails also provides environment-specific logging configurations. Since we're preparing for production, we'll add our customizations to the production configuration. Open racetrack/web-app/WEB-INF/log4j.production.properties and add the following configuration entries.

```
log4j.appender.access=org.apache.log4j.FileAppender
log4j.appender.access.file=access.log
log4j.appender.access.layout=org.apache.log4j.PatternLayout
log4j.appender.access.layout.ConversionPattern=%d %p %x [%c] %m%n

log4j.logger.UserController=warn,access
log4j.additivity.UserController=false
```

This configuration first defines a new log4j appender that will write to a file named `access.log`. It then instructs log4j to use that file to record all warning level (or higher) events from the `UserController` class. (This configuration writes the log file to the application's root directory. In a production environment, you'll want to have a directory dedicated exclusively to your log files and configure your log4j settings accordingly.)

To try it out, enter `grails prod run-app` (to run with the production configuration) and navigate to http://localhost:8080/racetrack/user/login (or any secured area of the application) and enter a bogus user ID and/or password. You should see the following output in `racetrack/access.log`.

```
2006-10-28 16:25:29,239 WARN  [UserController] Shields
up!  Somebody's trying to hack through our rock-solid
DEFCON 1 security -- User ID - hacker, Password - letmein
```

Now, when some nefarious fiend tries to break in to our application, we'll have a handy record of their activity.

Deploying

It's time to deploy our project to a production application server, and we'll do so in just three short steps.

First, we need to tell our production application how to communicate with the production database. Let's update `racetrack/grails-app/conf/ProductionDataSource.groovy` with the necessary configuration data. (Note that you'll need to change the `username` and `password` to the appropriate values for your MySQL account.)

```
class ProductionDataSource {
    boolean pooling = true
    String dbCreate = "update"
    String url = "jdbc:mysql://localhost/racetrack_prod"
    String driverClassName = "com.mysql.jdbc.Driver"
    String username = "prod"
    String password = "wahoowa"
}
```

Once the application is configured to use the production database, we're ready to build the WAR. To do, so, we simply enter `grails war`, and Grails takes care of the rest.

```
racetrack> grails war
...
war:
     [echo] Packaging for environment 'production'
...
BUILD SUCCESSFUL
Total time: 6 seconds
racetrack> ls -l racetrack.war
-rw-r--r--  1 jason  jason  11760541 Oct 28 17:02
racetrack.war
```

Notice the output above that indicates the application is being built for the production environment. That is certainly the behavior we want in this particular situation, but there may be times when you want to build a WAR to deploy in a development or test environment as well. By default, the `grails war` command prepares the application using the production database configuration (in `ProductionDataSource.groovy`); however, we can simply include the target environment in the command (e.g., `grails dev war`) to produce a WAR using the configuration for that environment instead.[32]

Now that we have a WAR, we're free to deploy the application on any application server we choose. The exact steps needed to deploy the WAR will, of course, vary across application servers. We'll use the freely available JBoss Application Server[36] as the target server for this example. With JBoss, we simply copy the WAR into the server's deployment directory, and start the server.

```
racetrack> cp racetrack.war /Applications/jboss-
4.0.5/server/default/deploy/
racetrack> /Applications/jboss-4.0.5/bin/run.sh
22:23:50,934 INFO  [Server] Starting JBoss (MX
MicroKernel)...
...
22:24:13,069 INFO  [TomcatDeployer] deploy,
ctxPath=/racetrack,
warUrl=.../tmp/deploy/tmp7718racetrack-exp.war/
```

```
...
22:24:35,671 INFO  [Server] JBoss (MX MicroKernel)
[4.0.5] Started in 24s:726ms
```

That's it. The application is now deployed, started, and ready to process requests. Fire up your browser and have a look – http://someproductionserver:8080/racetrack/.

App Server Quirks

Every application server has its quirks, and JBoss is no exception. If we want the application to log events properly when running in JBoss (in the same manner we established earlier), we have to jump through a few hoops. JBoss adopts the philosophy that the application server (not the application itself) should own the logging configuration. The following steps will bring us in line with that way of thinking.

1.   Remove the log4j-related artifacts from the WAR (so that we can use the corresponding JBoss log4j artifacts instead).

     • WEB-INF/log4j.properties
     • WEB-INF/lib/log4j-1.2.8.jar

2.   Edit the JBoss log4j configuration file –
     $JBOSS_HOME/server/default/conf/log4j.xml — to include the logging configuration for our application.

```
<appender name="RACETRACK"
class="org.jboss.logging.appender.DailyRollingFileAppender">
  <errorHandler
class="org.jboss.logging.util.OnlyOnceErrorHandler"/>
  <param name="File"
value="${jboss.server.log.dir}/racetrack.log"/>
  <param name="Append" value="false"/>

  <!-- Rollover at midnight each day -->
  <param name="DatePattern" value="'.'yyyy-MM-dd"/>

  <layout class="org.apache.log4j.PatternLayout">
     <!-- The default pattern: Date Priority [Category] Message\n
-->
     <param name="ConversionPattern" value="%d %-5p [%c] %m%n"/>
  </layout>
     </appender>
```

```
<category name="UserController">
    <priority value="WARN" />
    <appender-ref ref="RACETRACK"/>
</category>
```

Once these changes are in place, we can once again use the log file to keep track of any noteworthy events.

```
racetrack> cat /Applications/jboss-
4.0.5/server/default/log/racetrack.log
2006-10-28 22:40:09,174 WARN  [UserController] Shields
up!  Somebody's trying to hack through our rock-solid
DEFCON 1 security -- User ID - admin, Password - letmein
```

9

Tips and Tricks for Moving Forward

Every project is unique, and your needs are sure to differ in some way or another from the examples we've seen so far. The following sections cover some of the more common deviations as well as tips for dealing with the corresponding questions that arise. We'll also look at a few generally useful tips for moving forward with Grails.

Defining Your Own Database Tables

The approach we used in the *RaceTrack* example helped us quickly assemble our application, but we sometimes want a bit more control over certain details of our database tables (e.g., column sizes, constraints, partitions, etc.). We don't have to let Grails create the database tables for us. Grails will happily use a schema we define manually, and no additional configuration is necessary, so long as we follow the Grails naming conventions. (If we really want to color outside of the lines, we'll talk about integrating with non-conforming schemas in the next section.)

To tell Grails we want to manage the database tables on our own, simply remove (or comment out) the dbcreate property in the *DataSource classes and read on below for more information on the Grails conventions.

```
class DevelopmentDataSource {
    boolean pooling = true
    String dbCreate = "update"
    String url = "jdbc:mysql://localhost/racetrack_dev"
    String driverClassName = "com.mysql.jdbc.Driver"
    String username = "jason"
    String password = ""
}
```

Domain Classes and Table Names

First and foremost, the Grails conventions expect that you'll have a table for each domain class. As we saw in the *RaceTrack* application, the `Race` domain class mapped to the `race` table, the `Registration` domain class used the `registration` table, and so on. If you define your tables and domain classes using this pattern, Grails will let you skip any configuration work in this area. (If your domain classes happen to involve an inheritance hierarchy, then you'll want to check out the Grails wiki for more information on the Grails table-per-hierarchy model.[37])

Properties and Columns

Intuitively enough, Grails looks for a one-to-one mapping between domain class properties and database columns. For single-word properties, the property name will exactly match the column name. For example, the `name` property in the `Race` class mapped to the `name` column in the `race` table. For multi-word properties, Java naming conventions dictate the property name, and Grails conventions call for an underscore to separate each word in the column name. For example, the `startDateTime` property mapped to the `start_date_time` column.

We have some flexibility when it comes to the specific data types and sizes used for a column. For example, we can map a String object to a `CHAR(4)` column, a `VARCHAR(255)` column, a `TEXT` column, etc. We have similar leeway with numeric types. Of course, as the developer, we're responsible for defining proper constraints to make sure the domain class doesn't attempt to save data that cannot be successfully persisted to the database.

Lastly, we have the option of specifying which columns are nullable. We're free to be as restrictive or liberal as we please in this regard; we simply have to make sure our domain class constraints will prevent the application from trying to persist a null property value into a non-nullable database column.

Identity, Relationships, and Keys

GORM supplies each Grails domain class with an `id` and `version` property, and Grails expects each table to have columns of the same name. Both columns should be defined as integer types, and the `id` column should serve as the primary key for the table. (The exact type and size of the integer column used is at the developer's discretion. Just be sure to choose a size large enough to support the amount of data and activity you expect for your system.)

Grails follows an equally intuitive approach for handling relationships. For example, in the *RaceTrack* application, each `Registration` object belonged to a particular `Race` object. Grails therefore expects the `registration` table to include a `race_id` column, which acts as a foreign key to the `race` table.

Working with a Legacy Database Schema

Without a doubt, you'll get the maximum productivity benefit from Grails when working with a greenfield application where you can follow the Grails conventions. After all, one of the core premises behind Grails is a strong favoring of convention over configuration. Nevertheless, many applications will not have the luxury of defining a new database schema. Particularly in enterprise applications, we often find ourselves integrating with a legacy database schema, and changing the schema typically isn't an option. Luckily, Grails doesn't leave us out in the cold. Even with our legacy schema, we can still benefit from much of the Grails goodness we saw in the *RaceTrack* application.

To use Grails with a non-conforming schema, we have to revert to configuration. We need to tell Grails how to map our domain classes to our tables, how to map properties to columns, and how to uniquely identify each record. Fortunately, we have a few options for performing this mapping. For those privileged enough to have option of using Java 5, you can use Hibernate annotations to provide the mapping.[38] For the JDK 1.4 crowd, you'll want to use the equally-viable Hibernate XML for the mapping.[39]

ORM Troubleshooting

If you do find yourself working with a legacy schema or even if you just get into some complex relationships or queries, you may occasionally find that your application is not providing the exact results that you're expecting. In this case, it's a good idea to make sure that the object-relational mapping is doing what you expect under the hood. To do so, you can enable SQL logging by setting the `logSql` property to `true` in your data source.

```
class DevelopmentDataSource {
    def logSql = true
    boolean pooling = true
    String dbCreate = "update" // one of 'create',
                              'create-drop', 'update'
    String url = "jdbc:mysql://localhost/racetrack_dev"
    String driverClassName = "com.mysql.jdbc.Driver"
    String username = "jason"
    String password = ""
}
```

With SQL logging enabled, you'll now be able to see the format of the SQL the system is generating. For example, if we perform a query from the *Search for Races* page, we'll see the following output in the console.

```
[groovy] Hibernate:
    [groovy] select
    [groovy]     this_.id as id1_0_,
    [groovy]     this_.version as version1_0_,
    [groovy]     this_.distance as distance1_0_,
    [groovy]     this_.max_runners as max4_1_0_,
    [groovy]     this_.start_date_time as start5_1_0_,
    [groovy]     this_.state as state1_0_,
    [groovy]     this_.cost as cost1_0_,
    [groovy]     this_.name as name1_0_,
    [groovy]     this_.city as city1_0_
    [groovy]     from
    [groovy]         race this_
    [groovy]     where
    [groovy]     (
    [groovy]         this_.city like ?
    [groovy]         and this_.state like ?
    [groovy]         and this_.start_date_time between ? and ?
    [groovy]     )
```

All database activity – create, read, update, and delete – will now appear in the console. If you're trying to figure out why a certain property doesn't seem to load properly or why a particular query appears to ignore some of its parameters, the SQL logging output is a good place to begin your debugging effort. Because you know what you've asked the application to do, seeing the application's translation of that request into SQL will often provide that missing piece of information needed to help you address the problem.

Upgrading Grails

The Grails development team has established an aggressive road map for the framework.[40] We can expect regular improvements delivered in the form of minor releases every couple months, and we'll often want to upgrade our Grails applications to take advantage of the new features available in the latest release. With Grails, this too, is a simple process.

As a general precaution, you'll always want to make sure you have a backup of your application before you perform the upgrade. (Of course, having reliable backups isn't specific to this process. You are using a source code management system, right?)

Naturally, you first need to download and install the updated version of Grails. Then, you simply navigate to your project's root directory and issue the grails upgrade command.

```
racetrack> grails upgrade
...
BUILD SUCCESSFUL
Total time: 1 second
```

Congratulations, you're now running the latest version of Grails. Now go do something great with all those new features!

10

Summary

Over the course of this book, we've seen first-hand how we can use Grails to build a fully-functioning and flexible web application in minimal time. Groovy's highly-expressive nature allowed us to write concise code, and Grails's use of sensible defaults (à la convention over configuration) saved us from much of the coding and configuration we'd otherwise face with many traditional frameworks. Of course, writing less code also means that we have less code to maintain going forward. And, as the requirements continue to evolve over time, we'll have fewer lines of code to wade through to get our job done.

We've followed a very iterative – perhaps even agile – development approach to get to this point, and we've seen that Grails is well-suited to that development style.[41] That approach allows us to continuously see our progress as we develop the application and, in turn, opens the door to quicker feedback from our customers. We may not have made it to the golf course by 10 a.m., but a happy customer might just take us out for a round tomorrow.

And there's still more to Grails than what we've seen here. The Grails home page (http://grails.org) always has the latest news and updates. If you want to dig deeper and learn about Grails services, Ajax support (including the Prototype, Dojo, and Yahoo UI libraries), job scheduling, transaction management, JEE integration, etc., you'll find all that information and more on the Grails site as well. And, if for some reason you can't find what you're looking for, be sure to send a note to the increasingly-active user mailing list.[42]

Web development doesn't have to be a slow and cumbersome process; with Grails, rapid web application development on the Java platform has now arrived.

About the Author

Jason Rudolph is an Application Architect at Railinc, where he develops software to help trains move more efficiently throughout North America. He recently delivered an industry-wide inspection reporting and management system relied on for operational safety by Fortune 500 railroads, equipment leasing companies, and the Federal Railroad Administration.

Jason specializes in applying sound software engineering practices to solve hard problems and meet real business challenges. Jason has experience building several large-scale enterprise applications using JEE to interface with business partners, legacy back-end systems, and web-based users, and to provide scalable solutions for high transactional throughput. He enjoys working as a designer, an architect, and a developer, and believes that the real satisfaction comes from the hands-on coding that turns the blueprints into a working and useful application.

Jason's interests include dynamic languages, lightweight development methodologies, improving developer productivity, and a quest to keep programming fun. It's these interests that led Jason to become a Grails committer and evangelist. Jason holds a degree in Computer Science from the University of Virginia. He currently lives in Raleigh, NC with his wife (who can take a functional web app and make it actually look good) and his dog (who can outrun him, but is no match for squirrels). You can find Jason online at http://jasonrudolph.com.

Resources

[1] http://www.jcp.org/en/jsr/detail?id=241
Check out the official details of the Groovy spec (i.e., JSR 241: The Groovy Programming Language).

[2] http://groovy.codehaus.org/
The Groovy site is your official source for all things Groovy. Here you'll find information on downloading and installing Groovy, tutorials, APIs, FAQs, documentation, news, and more.

[3] http://infoq.com/minibooks/grails
This ZIP file includes the complete source code for all the examples in this book, with each folder containing a snapshot of the source as it exists at the end of a particular chapter.

[4] http://java.sun.com/javase/downloads/
Sun's Java Standard Edition download page offers JDK distributions for just about every platform under the sun.

[5] http://grails.org/Download
The Grails download page always offers the current stable Grails release as well as a snapshot of the upcoming release.

The examples in this book *should* work fine with future Grails releases; however, for best results, I recommend using one of the Grails 0.3.1 distributions below for developing the examples as you read along.

http://dist.codehaus.org/grails/grails-bin-0.3.1.tar.gz
http://dist.codehaus.org/grails/grails-bin-0.3.1.zip

[6] http://grails.org/Installation
The Grails installation instructions will have you up and running in no time.

[7] http://dev.mysql.com/downloads/mysql/5.0.html

Download and install MySQL Community Server 5.0 for all your
development needs. You can't beat the price!

[8] http://grails.org/Quick+Start#QuickStart-CreateaGrailsproject
The Grails *Quick Start* guide provides the official word on the structure of a
Grails application.

[9] http://en.wikipedia.org/wiki/DRY
This Wikipedia entry explains the essence of the DRY principle.

[10] http://grails.org/GORM+-+Defining+relationships#GORM-
Definingrelationships-RelationshipSummary
The GORM documentation lists a quick summary of the various relationship
types supported in Grails and the keywords associated with each type.

[11] http://www.mysql.com/products/connector/j/
MySQL Connector/J provides the JDBC drivers needed to interact with your
MySQL databases from a Grails application (or any Java or Groovy
application).

[12] http://grails.org/Validation+Reference
As you start to add constraints to your Grails application, be sure to
bookmark this page. The Grails *Validation Reference* guide lists all of the
available constraints, explains their usage, and provides the information you
need for customizing error messages as well.

[13] http://groovy.codehaus.org/Closures
The Groovy site's introduction to closures provides a detailed and helpful
explanation of the purpose, syntax, and semantics of Groovy closures. It
includes several handy examples, and even touches on the differences
between closures, code blocks, and anonymous inner classes.

[14] http://groovy.codehaus.org/GroovyMarkup
Groovy Markup provides a convenient mechanism for using Groovy to build
XML, HTML, Hibernate Criteria, etc.

[15] http://grails.org/Validation#Validation-ValidatingDomainClasses
This section of the Grails documentation explains how to define a constraints
closure and how to use the `validate` and `save` methods on Grails domain
classes.

[16] http://grails.org/Validation+Reference#ValidationReference-validator
In addition to the many standard Grails validators, the Grails *Validation
Reference* guide also describes how to define and use custom validators.

[17] http://groovy.codehaus.org/apidocs/groovy/lang/GString.html
The Groovy GString API lists the many handy methods provided by this class, some examples of its use, and a quick mention of how it got its rather clever name.

[18] http://grails.org/Controllers#Controllers-Settingthedefaultaction
Grails offers two options for setting the default action on a controller.

[19]

http://grails.org/Dynamic+Methods+Reference#DynamicMethodsReference-Controllers
Grails controllers offer numerous dynamic methods and properties for everything from accessing the request and the session, to logging, to implementing a redirect, and everything in between.

[20]

http://grails.org/Dynamic+Methods+Reference#DynamicMethodsReference-DomainClasses
Not to be outdone by Grails controllers, Grails domain classes provide dynamic properties and methods that are sure to save you hours of burdensome ORM work.

[21] http://grails.org/GSP+Tag+Reference
The *GSP Tag Reference* guide identifies the various Grails tags available for working with forms, validation, Ajax, etc. For each tag, the documentation explains the tag's API and offers examples of its use.

[22] http://grails.org/Tag+-+datePicker
The datePicker tag renders a UI widget for selecting a date/time value and offers options for controlling the precision of the value.

[23] http://grails.org/Builders#Builders-HibernateCriteriaBuilder
The Hibernate Criteria Builder provides a convenient mechanism for performing all sorts of queries on your domain model.

[24] http://en.wikipedia.org/wiki/Polish_notation
The true computer science geeks will no doubt have fond memories of developing expressions in Polish notation. Just don't try to communicate with mortals using this syntax.

[25] http://groovy.codehaus.org/Roadmap#Roadmap-Groovy2.0
The Groovy roadmap gives us an idea of what we can expect in future Groovy releases, including support for enumerations in Groovy 2.0.

[26] http://en.wikipedia.org/wiki/SHA

Wikipedia offers a thorough explanation of the Secure Hash Algorithm (SHA), its various flavors, and why it can serve as a good choice for most encryption needs.

[27] http://java.sun.com/j2se/1.5.0/docs/api/java/security/MessageDigest.html
If you're ready to lock down your application and you're rolling your own authentication module, then check out Java's `MessageDigest` API for its one-way hashing functions.

[28] http://grails.org/Configuration#Configuration-ConfiguringStartup
The Grails documentation includes an explanation of the bootstrap functionality for defining application start-up and tear-down tasks.

[29] http://grails.org/Controllers#Controllers-ActionInterceptors
Grails action interceptors allow you to inject additional code to execute before or after a Grails action.

[30] http://grails.org/Views+and+Layouts#ViewsandLayouts-LayoutbyConvention
As an alternative to referencing layouts by name (as demonstrated in the *RaceTrack* example), Grails also allows you to use a convention-based approach to determining the layout associated with a given view.

[31] http://groovy.codehaus.org/Unit+Testing
Groovy notably simplifies unit testing on the Java platform. The Groovy *Unit Testing* page includes just a few examples of how Groovy can help speed up your test case development.

[32] http://grails.org/Configuration#Configuration-Environments
Grails allows you to specify the environment you want to use for various commands and includes logical defaults for each command as well.

[33] http://grails.org/Functional+Testing
In addition to the unit testing framework, the Grails functional testing framework will help you further maintain the quality of your application as you aggressively progress through your development iterations.

[34]
http://grails.org/Controller+Dynamic+Methods#ControllerDynamicMethods-log
Find out how to access and customize the logging functionality available in Grails controllers.

[35] http://logging.apache.org/log4j/docs/documentation.html

Because Grails logging uses log4j, you can take advantage of log4j's superb flexibility to tailor the logging functionality to your specific needs.

[36] http://labs.jboss.com/portal/jbossas/download
Download and install JBoss Application Server for a free and production-capable deployment solution.

[37] http://www.grails.org/GORM+-+Mapping+inheritance
The GORM documentation explains how domain class inheritance affects ORM.

[38] http://grails.org/Hibernate+Integration#HibernateIntegration-MappingwithHibernateAnnotations
Hibernate annotations allow developers to use Grails for their applications even when working with a non-standard database schema.

[39] http://jasonrudolph.com/blog/2006/06/20/hoisting-grails-to-your-legacy-db/
If your environment doesn't yet support annotations (i.e., you're using JDK 1.4), you can still hook Grails up to your legacy database schemas using Hibernate XML for the mapping.

[40] http://grails.org/Roadmap
The Grails roadmap lays out the many features and improvements you can expect in each upcoming release and provides an estimated timeline for those releases as well.

[41] http://www.amazon.com/exec/obidos/ASIN/0131111558/
Craig Larman's book, *Agile and Iterative Development: A Manager's Guide*, serves as a great introduction to Agile Development.

[42] http://www.nabble.com/grails---user-f11861.html
The Grails user mailing list archives are fully-searchable and provide a great source for answers to all sorts of questions. You can also feel free to post your own questions or comments to the mailing list, and chances are, you'll receive a fairly timely reply.

www.ingramcontent.com/pod-product-compliance
Lightning Source LLC
Chambersburg PA
CBHW021144070326
40689CB00043B/1125